PRAISE FOR JASON LEWIS AND

THE SEED BURIED DEEP

"An adventure of two lifetimes."
—*SAN FRANCISCO CHRONICLE*

"*The Expedition* speaks powerfully of a reality most people need to hear. It takes noble thinking on behalf of the planet, a love for life, and a soul full of dreams to accomplish a truly great journey."
—*LES STROUD, Survivorman*

"A catalogue of hair-raising adventures."
—*PRESS ASSOCIATION*

"The perfect blend of action, tragedy, humor and suspense. In the first chapter alone. A must read."
—*ADVENTURE CYCLIST*

"In an age of SUVs, jumbo jets, and luxury cruise liners, Jason Lewis proves we can go anywhere in the world using only the power of our own two feet, including around it."
—*DAVID TEMPLEMAN-ADAMS, first person to reach the Geographic and Magnetic North and South Poles*

"We need the Lewises of this life. It is good to know that such people exist, have always existed, doubtless always will exist. It does our hearts good to hear about them."
—*THE LONDON TIMES*

THE
EXPEDITION

TRUE STORY OF THE FIRST HUMAN-POWERED
CIRCUMNAVIGATION OF THE EARTH

2 THE SEED BURIED DEEP

Withdrawn from Stock

JASON LEWIS

BILLYFISH
BOOKS

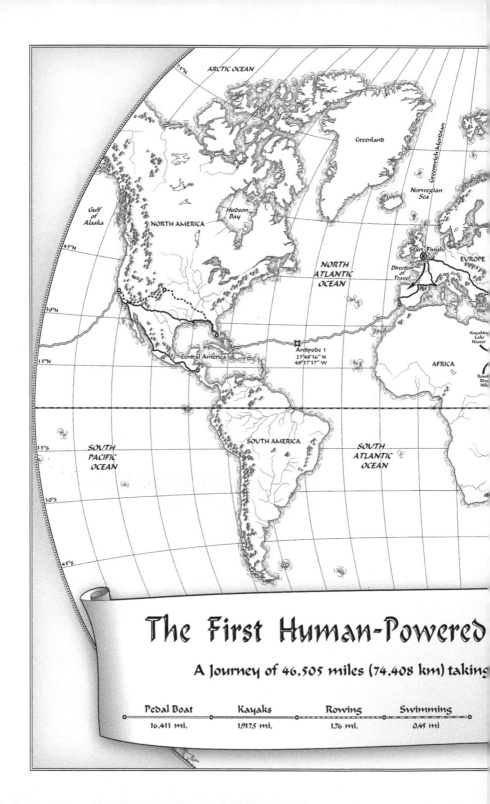

ARCTIC OCEAN

Greenland

Norwegian
Sea

Gulf
of
Alaska

NORTH AMERICA

Hudson
Bay

45°N

Start/Finish

EUROPE

NORTH
ATLANTIC
OCEAN

Direction
of
Travel

30°N

Antipode 1
25°48'16" N
48°37'37" W

15°N

Central America

AFRICA

15°S

SOUTH AMERICA

SOUTH
PACIFIC
OCEAN

SOUTH
ATLANTIC
OCEAN

30°S

45°S

The First Human-Powered

A Journey of 46,505 miles (74,408 km) taking

Pedal Boat	Kayaks	Rowing	Swimming
16,411 mi.	1,917.5 mi.	1.76 mi.	0.45 mi

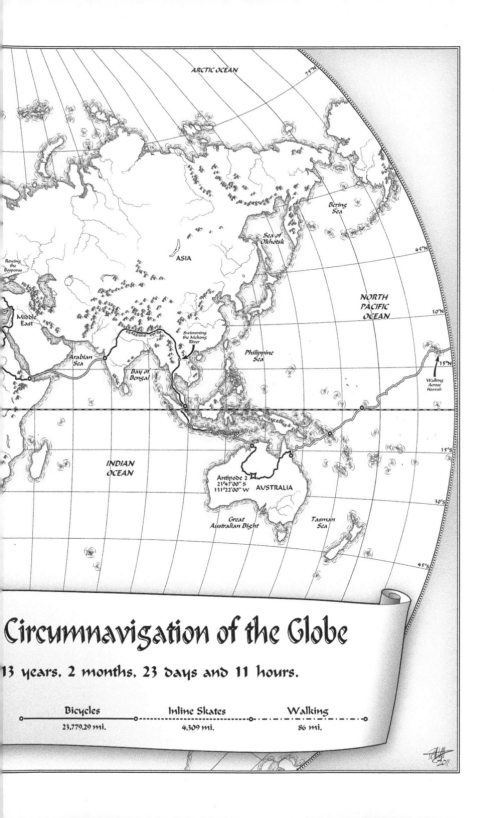

ARCTIC OCEAN

Bering
Sea

Sea of
Okhotsk

ASIA

Rowing
the
Bosporus

NORTH
PACIFIC
OCEAN

Middle
East

Swimming
the Mekong
River

Arabian
Sea

Philippine
Sea

Bay of
Bengal

Walking
Across
Hawaii

INDIAN
OCEAN

Antipode 2
23°47'00" S
131°22'00" W   AVSTRALIA

Great
Australian Bight

Tasman
Sea

Circumnavigation of the Globe

13 years, 2 months, 23 days and 11 hours.

Bicycles	Inline Skates	Walking
23,779.29 mi.	4,309 mi.	86 mi.

First BillyFish Books edition 2014

For permission requests, write to the publisher: permissions@billyfishbooks.com
www.billyfishbooks.com

ISBN 978-0-9849155-1-4 (pbk.)

British Library Cataloguing in Publication Data. A catalogue record for this book is available from the British Library.

Publisher's Cataloging-in-Publication data
Lewis, Jason, 1967 -.
The seed buried deep : true story of the first human-powered circumnavigation of the earth
/ Jason Lewis.
p. cm.
ISBN 978-0-9849155-1-4
Series : The Expedition.
1. Lewis, Jason, 1967 - --Travel. 2. Adventure travel. 3. Voyages and travels. 4. Voyages around the world. 5. Human powered vehicles. 6. Spirituality. I. Title. II. Series.
G465 .L495 2013
910.4 --dc23   2012902558

All wood product components used in print versions of this book meet Sustainable Forestry Initiative® (SFI®) Certified Sourcing (USA) and Forest Stewardship Council™ (FSC®) Mixed Credit (UK) standards.

Cover photograph © Kenny Brown
Maps © Rob Antonishen/Cartocopia
Cover design by Kevin Jones

10 9 8 7 6 5 4 3 2 1

SYNOPSIS

This is the second instalment of *The Expedition* trilogy.

In his first book, *Dark Waters*, window cleaner Jason Lewis teams up with former college friend, environmentalist Steve Smith, to attempt the first human-powered circumnavigation of the Earth. Aided by Steve's father, Stuart, a fun-loving insurance salesman with the gift of the gab, filmmaker Kenny Brown, Scotland's answer to MacGyver, and a loyal band of oddball volunteers, the unlikely duo struggle to attract sponsors. After two years, with little to show for themselves but bungled sea trials, run-ins with the police, and a humiliating inaugural press event, the aspiring adventurers set off anyway, biking from the Greenwich meridian. Low on funding but high on hope, world maps and oceanic charts in tow, they immediately become lost having forgotten to bring a London A to Z street atlas.

From Rye, they manage an illegal crossing of the Channel to Boulogne in their one-of-a-kind craft, *Moksha*, constructed by first-time boat builders Chris and Hugo. Next, they wheel south through Europe, visiting schools along the way, using the expedition to champion world citizenship and environmental responsibility.

Their determination and friendship are put to the test during a gruelling 111-day crossing of the Atlantic. Early on they are nearly crushed by a rogue trawler, and Jason suffers hypoxia when he almost drowns. They endure extreme fatigue, painful salt sores, bitter disagreements, and a monster wave that capsizes the boat, throwing Steve overboard. But their ruthless initiation is also tempered by occasional forays into the sublime: resplendent sunsets, fathomless night skies, and a surprise Christmas dinner served by a passing ship. In the closing stages of the voyage, following months of meditative contemplation, Jason undergoes a life-changing transformation: a spiritual epiphany providing a comforting glimpse into the interconnectedness of all life.

The peace isn't to last, however.

After running aground on a reef in the Caribbean and a brush with Cuban pirates, our fledgling explorers stumble ashore in Miami. They face months of monotonous fundraising before resuming their journey separately across the US, giving each other much needed space before the longer Pacific voyage. Steve bikes through the Southern states while Jason learns to rollerblade on a more northerly route to San Francisco. He falls foul of ravenous fire ants, parsimonious Baptists, and gun-toting rednecks who take exception to his long hair and unorthodox choice of travel. Nevertheless, it is in the hospitality of strangers that he discovers another America, one where those less fortunate are often the first to offer food and shelter.

At the end of an exhausting 70-mile skate across the Eastern Plains of Colorado, complete with thunderstorms and sexual solicitations, Jason enters the town of Pueblo and becomes the victim of a brutal hit and run.

We pick up the story in *The Seed Buried Deep* with Jason lying by the side of the road, both his legs horribly broken.

CONTENTS

For Tammie

And the sacrifices you've made to bring this story

kicking and screaming into the world

When you call yourself an Indian or a Muslim or a Christian or a European, or anything else, you are being violent. Why? Because you are separating yourself from the rest of mankind. When you separate yourself by belief, by nationality, by tradition, it breeds violence.

—Jiddu Krishnamurti, *Freedom from the Known*

Ah've never felt a fuckin thing aboot countries, other than total disgust. They should abolish the fuckin lot ay them. Kill every fuckin parasite politician that ever stood up and mouthed lies and fascist platitudes in a suit and a smarmy smile.

—Irvine Welsh, *Trainspotting*

Highway 50, Pueblo, Colorado. September 10, 1995

A MILE UP THE road from where I lay, legs horribly broken, a battered Nissan pickup pulled in front of a silver Cadillac, forcing it to stop. A Hispanic man with a pencil moustache stepped out and approached the larger vehicle. Passing motorists might have thought a carjacking was in progress. This was Dogpatch, after all, an area of town renowned for violent crime. In actual fact, Ed Apodaca was terrified. He and his young daughter had just witnessed a brutal hit and run—the Caddy ploughing into a lone figure skating along the hard shoulder, scooping up the body and flinging it over the roof like a rag doll.

Ed feared the worst. These people were clearly desperate, in all probability gangbangers out joyriding. Shooting the only eyewitnesses to manslaughter would mean nothing to them. He peered through a hole in the shattered windscreen, expecting to see a gun levelled at him. An elderly couple blinked back instead.

"Jesus!" Ed exclaimed, his trepidation turning to anger. "Do you have *any* idea what you've just done?"

Wilbur Ladd's hands were trembling against the steering wheel. His wife had my backpack in her lap. "We thought we'd hit a deer," she whispered.

"OH MY GOD! Oh my God!"

I came to with a lightly built man standing over me, gaping at my legs in horror. How long had I been lying there? Five minutes? Ten? The shock of the impact was wearing off and barbs of molten pain coursed through my lower legs.

Ed knelt down beside me. "It's going to be okay, buddy. An ambulance is on its way." A bewildered-looking older man hovered behind him, shards of glass glinting on his evening jacket. Another motorist was talking urgently into a mobile phone.

Minutes passed. Ed kept me talking. "Where are you from? Where are you headed?" A highway patrol car pulled up, lights flashing. After giving Wilbur a friendly handshake, the officer strolled over to where I was sprawled, tibias protruding, and started scribbling on a pad.

"You were skating on the wrong side of the highway."[*] His voice was flat and emotionless. "What's your address?"

It had been a long day: gut-wrenching feedlots, pasty-faced crackpots offering blowjobs, and being left for dead with two broken legs by an eighty-two-year-old drunk driver with cataracts.[†] Incurring a fine was the last straw.

I closed my eyes and said nothing. The pain was becoming unbearable.

"I need an address," the cop repeated impatiently. "Else I'll be writing another citation for vagrancy."

Is this guy being serious? I thought. *Prick should be a comedian.*

"He's with me," Ed suddenly interjected. "You can use my address."

This Good Samaritan barely knew me, yet here he was volunteering his address for a ticket I had no intention of paying.

Sirens interrupted the farce, an ambulance turning the faces around me blue, orange, and white. Two paramedics in fluorescent yellow jackets took over, gentle fingers probing my head, neck, and spine before rolling me onto a stretcher. A needle prick in both thighs, and the dulling effect of morphine began spreading throughout my lower body. Next thing I was on a gurney being shunted into the back of the ambulance.

I roused from the narcotic haze to find Ed sitting beside me. The ambulance was still stationary.

---

[*] In 1995, skaters were classified as pedestrians in Pueblo County.

[†] The Ladds were on their way back from a function at the Masonic Lodge where Wilbur was Worshipful Master. In his deposition, Ed Apodaca described smelling alcohol on Mr Ladd's breath, something the police officer conveniently neglected to test for. It also transpired that Wilbur was scheduled for a cataract operation. He subsequently lost his driving licence.

"What's the hold-up?" I asked groggily.

"Your ear almost got torn off. They're just making sure they don't leave any of you behind."

A *Far Side* cartoon flashed to mind: some scavenging mongrel making off with a random body part in its mouth, paramedics in hot pursuit.

Eventually, all appendages accounted for, the doors closed and the ambulance picked up speed. Then I remembered something. It was Steve's birthday. *What would he say if he saw me now?* I wondered.

"I told you so," probably.

COLORADO
FRESH BLOOD ON THE ROAD

Out here a man wasn't judged by whether he could read or write, or what his color was, or what kind of family he came from, or how much money he had back there, but by his skill … his mountain craft.

—WIN BLEVINS, *Give Your Heart to the Hawks,*
A Tribute to the Mountain Men

I AWOKE REINCARNATED INTO a world of tubes. Tubes in my arms, fingers, legs, nose, and penis—every hole, it seemed, apart from my bunghole. The blips and wheezes of hospital machinery filled a room lit by sunlight. I felt a wave of nausea, and the sky blue walls and eggshell ceiling swam together. A nurse appeared with a bowl just in time.

The room turned dark again.

The second time I awoke to voices.

"Good thing it was in his backpack," one was saying, his voice nasal sounding. "Probably saved his life when he hit the windshield." Then another, more familiar, and laughing: "I don't think he'll be doing anymore cooking with it, though!"

Stuart. What's he doing here?

The edges of the room slowly sharpened. A powerfully built man in blue scrubs had my cooking pot in his hands. It was crumpled flat, like it had been run over by a Mack Truck. Costing fifty cents from a thrift store in St Petersburg, the saucepan was the best life insurance policy I could have had, cushioning the force of the collision and preventing my spine from being shattered against the windscreen.

The conversation became animated. Stuart, who I later learned had jumped on the first plane from Fort Lauderdale after learning of the accident, was pushing for a second opinion on the plan to hammer titanium rods through what remained of my tibias. Just as barbecue skewers hold pieces of meat together, so the rods would realign the shattered segments of my lower legs, long enough for the bones to knit back together—hopefully.

Reminding me of an eagle with his beaky, schoolmasterly expression, Doctor Ken Danylchuk seemed more amused than anything by the cross-examination. He was one of the finest orthopaedic surgeons in the state, yet here was this Brit, familiar only with the antiquated methods of the National Health Service, challenging his expert opinion.

"Okay, Doctor Stuart!" he chuckled. "You're the boss. I'll see if I can't get one of my colleagues to look at the x-rays for your ... second opinion."

This was the beginning of it, a special connection forged in the slash and cauterized burn of the operating room, and fortified during Ken's daily rounds of the intensive care unit. Most days, the talk would digress from the state of my legs, to the state of world rugby, and inevitably to the state of the Colorado Avalanche ice hockey team rating for that season. Ken was Canadian. He had hockey on the brain.

Noticing that I was awake, he turned to me cheerfully and asked, "So how is Pueblo treating you, Jason?"

Was this a Canadian leg-pull? Despite being a resident of the US for many years, the expatriate had clearly kept a dry sense of humour.

"Great," I croaked. "The police have been especially generous."

Ken proceeded to inspect the blood-soaked dressings for signs of primary infection. The night of the accident he'd carried out an initial procedure to irrigate the open fractures, removing as much dirt and debris as possible. Risk of suppuration had to be minimized before inserting the interlocking rods. For the next three days I had to lie completely still. Any movement and the bones would grind against each other, causing excruciating pain.

"Looks like the fender hit your left leg first, midway between the ankle and the knee." The surgeon gestured with a rubber-gloved hand. "With any luck we'll have you up and skating again, Jason. But I'm obliged to warn you of the possibility of osteomyelitis."

"That doesn't sound good," said Stuart, the seriousness in his face complementing the creases in his trademark leather hat. "What is it?"

"Inflammation of the bone marrow," Ken explained.

"Can it be treated?"

"Depending on how advanced the infection is, we have pretty good results with antibiotics. But there can be complications."

"Such as?"

Ken hesitated. "Well, the infection can spread into the surrounding soft tissue. Worst-case scenario, your lower leg would have to be amputated. Otherwise gangrene could progress above the knee and we'd be looking at ..."

I wasn't listening anymore. All I heard was *gangrene* and *amputated*, words I'd only previously associated with healthcare in the Middle Ages. If I lost my leg, the expedition would surely be over for me. I would return to England crippled, unable to make a living even as a window cleaner. It was a dire prospect.

Later, though, lying in the darkness, imagining life as a uniped, I began thinking: *Paralympians go like the wind using wheelchairs. If I can do a mile in one, I can do the remaining 2,000 to San Francisco, given enough time—just like I did with the rollerblades.* But other doubts soon crowded in. *How long is Steve prepared to wait? Where will the money come from to pay the hospital bills? And even if I could afford a specially designed wheelchair, is it actually possible to scale the Rocky Mountains using just the power of my arms?*

ALERTED BY NANCY in Florida, Steve and Eilbhe arrived from Flagstaff on the evening of my fourth day in hospital. They looked fit, tanned, and very much in love. Eilbhe, a cascade of tumbling auburn curls framing her oval face, brought to mind a Celtic sprite of the woods. Raw, unembellished beauty wasn't her only gift, apparently.

"She can stand on one leg, fart, and whistle the Irish national anthem, all at the same time," Steve gushed with pride, entwining his arms around her and kissing her upraised forehead. I agreed that this was a rare talent indeed, warming instantly to her unassuming airs.

As conversation turned to the accident, I waited for the reprimand: *"Rollerblades. I told you so, Jason."*

It never came. "The main thing is you're alive, mate," Steve said gently, fixing me with his piercing stare. "I'll wait for you in San Francisco. It doesn't matter how long it takes, okay?"

Smiling weakly through the tangle of tubes, I felt my eyes well. *Steve's a loyal friend*, I thought. *A better friend to me than I've ever been to him.*

I WAS BED-BOUND for the next two weeks following successful insertion of the rods. Then the long rehabilitation process began. The first assignment from Eric, my rehab nurse, was to use a wheelchair to reach the bathroom. As well as relieving myself somewhere other than in my own bed, the thirty-foot round trip did away with the need for an electric leg exerciser to maintain blood circulation. This was a welcome development. The machine was set to elevate each leg thirty degrees above the horizontal, and Stuart had a knack of inadvertently knocking the dial, sending my feet to the ceiling and back.

Three weeks of racing wheelchairs around the fourth floor with another trauma patient, Jack, whose pelvis had been crushed by industrial machinery, and I was ready to be discharged. Wilbur Ladd's insurance covered the medical fees, a whopping $110,000. I owed Ed Apodaca more than my life. With no insurance of my own, the expedition would have been buried under a fresh mound of debt.

Ken and his wife Cathy extended a philanthropic offer for Stuart and me to stay at the family getaway, a 400-acre ranch nestled in the Front Range of the Rockies. It was now late October. The first autumn snows had fallen, dusting the trees and turning the foothills into a winter wonderland. Apart from the wind sighing through the ponderosa pines surrounding the cabin, I imagined it the quietest place on Earth.

When he wasn't busy seeing to my needs, Stuart was out in the pastures, often waist deep in snow, forking hay to eighty-one head of hungry North American bison. His tireless enthusiasm and good spirits were an inspiration to me. I, meanwhile, set about adapting to life at ground level, scooting around on my backside, the wheelchair being too wide to negotiate the cabin's narrow doorways. This made me a sitting duck for all the other short-arsed residents. My face was the perfect licking height for Wilson, Ken's beloved chocolate Labrador, and my back the perfect claw-sharpening angle for the two kittens. On weekends, my entire body became a climbing frame for Tyler, the Danylchuk's two-year-old son.

To stave off cabin fever, Stuart and I resumed our former team effort visiting schools. It was at nearby Rye Elementary where we first met April, a vivacious woman in her mid-forties with clear blue eyes and sweeping locks of silken hair. Only that week, her fifth-grade class had been studying early explorers, swashbuckling privateers like Vasco da Gama, Francisco Vasquez de Coronado, and the English hero-cum-pirate Sir Francis Drake. It was perfect timing for the children to see how adventuring had changed over the years, most notably in the cutlass and huge moustache department.

Living history was April's passion. She showed us some of her beloved Indian artefacts, including a tepee, explaining how hands-on teaching aids helped engage students with the nomadic culture of the Plains Indians. Tangible experience was the key to inspiring lifelong learners, she claimed. "Tell me, and I will forget. Show me, and I may remember. Involve me, and I'll understand."

I mentioned an upcoming presentation we had at the Colorado School for the Deaf and Blind. "Only problem is," I said anxiously, "how do we show the expedition route to kids who can't see?"

April thought about this for a minute. Then she said, "I have a cunning plan," a line I would hear her say many more times over the coming years.

Her class spent the next two weeks customizing a wall map of the world, gluing spaghetti to represent the outline of the continents, split peas for the expedition route, and different grades of sandpaper for a rudimentary braille key to illustrate the different modes of human power. As much a meal as a means of orientation by the time it was finished, the map was a huge hit on the day. Kids impaired both visually and aurally took turns piecing together a mental map of the expedition's planetary orbit, their fingers flitting across the textured surface like butterfly wings.

It was at this point I realized how an experienced educator like April, skilled at transcending communication barriers, could take the expedition to the next level in connecting children of different cultures.

By March, I'd graduated from a wheelchair to a wooden staff. My right leg was healing well, but a question mark still hung over the left. Having helped all he could, Nurse Stuart returned to Florida, while I moved nearer to District 60 schools in Pueblo. My new home became the spare room of a brick bungalow belonging to Dick and Sharon Conger, a modest, unassuming couple who'd befriended Stuart in Parkview Medical Center.

April and I met one afternoon at a coffee shop in town to discuss the world citizenship film for UNESCO. I began explaining, or rather complaining, about the lack of progress.

"Kenny can't afford to stay out on the road all the time," I grumbled. "The whole programme has basically ground to a halt."

April considered the dilemma. "What about getting the kids to do it using the expedition camcorder? I'm sure they'd love to make a video, especially if they know boys and girls their own age around the world will get to see it."

I was doodling with a spoon, excavating sludge from the bottom of my coffee cup. The idea of turning kids into filmmakers sounded almost too simple. It certainly contravened all rules for the time. In 1996, films were still shot by professional camera operators using pro gear, then cut by pro editors into programmes that looked polished and professional. Heaving convention out of the window would inevitably mean a drop in production standards, but promised a far more candid portrayal of children's lives than adults poking big scary cameras in their faces. The financial savings would also be huge.

"They'd need to learn a thing or two about operating the camera," I replied. "Like how to keep it steady and keeping their fingers off the zoom. Otherwise, though, why not? They could even help with the editing if we do it on a VHS system."

Within six weeks, we had our first video, a ten-minute glimpse into the life and times of a group of eleven-year-olds growing up in rural Colorado. The Spanish teacher at Rye High School translated subtitles for the schools we'd be visiting in Central and South America. As the circumnavigation progressed, films from other countries would be added to the exchange pool, allowing youngsters to "step into the world" of their global neighbours.*

The Video Exchange Program, as we named it, preserved the UNESCO theme of world citizenship, but the underlying philosophy ran deeper. "We are black," the Native American Chief Spokane Garry had once said, "yet if we cut ourselves, the blood will be red. And so with the whites it is the same, though their skin be white. I am of another nation. When I speak, you do not understand me. When you speak, I do not understand you."

Shortly before completing the Atlantic voyage, following months of meditative contemplation, I'd reached a similar conclusion during a transcendent state of non-dualistic awareness. At the height of *Samadhi*, my train of consciousness expanded faster and faster along a space-time continuum until an independent mind to witness reality ceased

---

* Distribution of films was something of a challenge in the pre-digital era. We carried VHS cassettes in our bicycle panniers and used the UNESCO Associated Schools Program Network to recruit schools. Photo album and pen pal exchange programmes were also launched for groups without access to a television and videocassette recorder.

to exist—the observer and the observed became one. Some time later, after being spat out through the cosmic rabbit hole to regular, dualistic experience, one insight overrode all: The differences between my so-called "self" and others were merely inventions of mind, labels shaped and skewed by consciousness, giving me, the host, a false sense of separateness. Beyond these illusions, only a common chemistry, pure energy, prevailed.

They're necessary illusions, of course, providing us with the means to navigate our surroundings: evaluate and respond, survive and prosper; five million years of hominid evolution producing the success story of *Homo sapiens*. But with natural selection in charge, where is it all heading? The predominant traits of neo-tribalism—war, persecution, bigotry, environmental exploitation—show little sign of abating as world population soars.

I told myself: As long as humans remain fooled by race, religion, language, culture, national identity, even personal identity, the species will continue to be at odds with itself. This was the real rationale behind the ten-minute films: for children, still free from the deceptions of adulthood, to hold a mirror to the world, and say, "Look, we are all One." Faced with a reflection of truer self, their global contemporaries would surely feel a broadening kinship and compassion to embrace the whole.

THE AMERICAN WEST
LEARNING HOW TO BREATHE AGAIN

Women are like tea bags. You never know how strong they are until you put them in hot water.

—ELEANOR ROOSEVELT

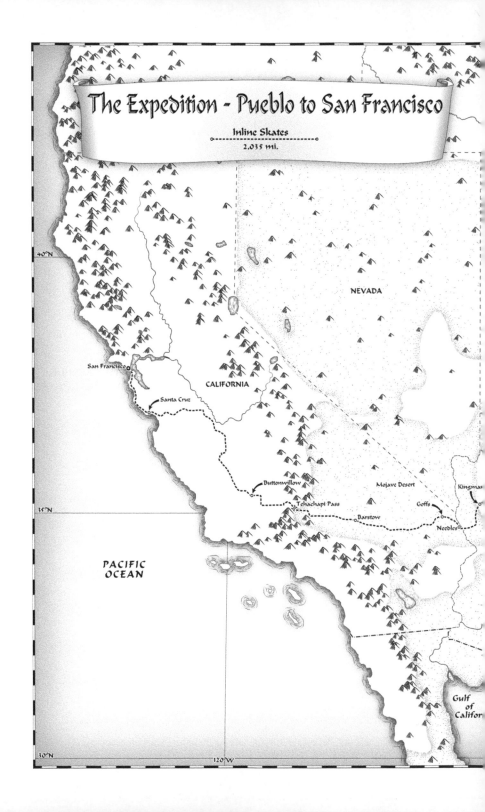

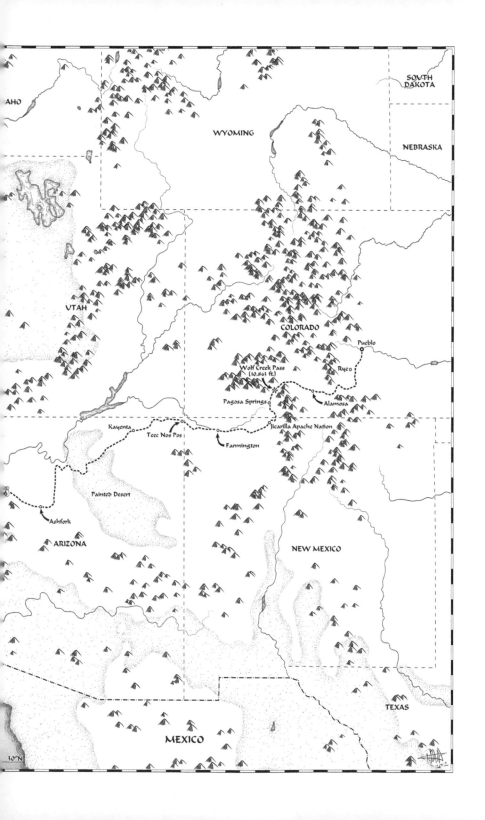

"SO HOW FAR HAVE you ridden before, April?"

I braced the handlebars while she tried jamming a second sleeping mat under a bungee cord already stretched to breaking point. A disorderly mound of tents, sleeping bags, water bottles, bike pumps, and other camping paraphernalia completely obscured the rear portion of her bike.

"Around seven miles," she replied nervously, pushing at the mat. A bead of sweat trickled out from under her grey baseball cap and disappeared behind a pair of aviator sunglasses. It was past noon and swelteringly hot. "And they've just been straight and level on the airstrip outside my house. Nothing with hills. Nothing with heat."

"Any concerns?"

Looking up, she brushed a strand of damp hair from her face and wrinkled her nose. "Hmm, hills intimidate me pretty good." In light of the fact our route would take us over one of the world's great mountain ranges, the Rockies, this struck me as unfortunate. "But when the going gets tough," she continued, breaking into a grin, "I'll just have to cowboy up."

We were on the shoulder of Highway 50, at the exact spot I'd been hit nine and a half months earlier. Every time a vehicle hurtled past, I flinched—a flashback of the impact slamming against my mental retina. Numerous treatments to stimulate knitting between the bone fragments in my left leg, including physiotherapy, osteopathy, electric pulse, comfrey infusions, and magnets, had all proved ineffective. In May, Doctor Ken proposed a third operation to re-break the tibia and graft bone from my hip. It would have meant starting from scratch. Another nine months of recuperation. Another nine months of Steve twiddling his thumbs in San Francisco. Both were inconceivable. With the titanium rod doing the job of the left tibia, it was either take a crack at the West Coast now, or suggest Steve choose another expedition partner.

Supporting a fully laden backpack would be pushing it, though. And so, a month before setting out, I'd asked April if she knew of a cyclist willing to schlep my gear the first 200 miles to Pagosa Springs, possibly further depending on how my legs fared. Having a rider along would serve another useful purpose. If I managed to scale Wolf Creek Pass, twelve miles of sheer incline, I could control my speed on the downhill side by braking against the back of the bike.

"I'll do it," she'd replied enthusiastically.

This threw me. April fit the role of seasoned adventurer about as convincingly as Britney Spears playing Hamlet. Blonde, a little ditsy on occasion, she lived on a cattle ranch and taught in a small, well-heeled Christian community where lace curtains twitched at the mere suggestion of anyone singing from a different hymn sheet. *No*, I said to myself, *I need someone with experience. Someone who won't give up on the second day after the romantic appeal has worn off.*

Then again, who was I to talk? Steve and I had human-powered our way nearly a third of the way around the planet with only the haziest notion of what we were doing. Why not April?

I steadied the bicycle long enough for my new travelling companion to step over the centre frame and push off. For the first thirty feet, April bunny-hopped on one foot while I skated behind, continuing to balance the woefully overladen rig. Reservations came flooding back. *Maybe I was wrong to assume we'd make it through the first day. At this rate we'll be lucky to make it through the first five minutes ...*

Then the bike picked up speed, the handlebars stopped wobbling, and we were on our way.

As we turned south on Interstate 25 towards Walsenburg, the shoulder changed to the dreaded band-aid surface. High-voltage shocks were shooting up each leg as I pushed forward over the uneven gravel chips. And when it started to rain, and April took her first spill, sending our sleeping bags bouncing under an eighteen-wheeler, I thought: *That's it. At least we tried.*

I lifted the tangle of spokes and equipment off April's 100-pound frame, retrieved the video camera, and filled the viewfinder with her scarlet face.

"Okay, April. Ready to call it quits?"

Trucks roared past unnervingly close, tyres hissing on the wet tarmac. Black clouds scudded overhead, sucking light from the sky and turning the scene even gloomier.

April, sodden hair plastered over her ears like seaweed, flashed a brilliant smile. "Oh no," she said brightly. "This is my greatest adventure!"

The woman's certifiable, I thought. *Any normal person would have called for a taxi by now.*

THE ROAD LEADING west out of South Fork is treacherous, a narrow two-laner with no shoulder that snakes through a river gorge veiled in shadow. Vertical cliffs rear up either side, the walls of metamorphic rock fixed with netting to hold back rockslides.

"It's all about technique going uphill on rollerblades," I panted into the camera (I was filming my skates pointing out at herringbone angles to the mountain grade). "If you get the right technique, it's actually not that hard at all." I chuckled to myself. "Only problem is I don't have the technique!"

Behind me, April's legs were spinning like egg beaters. She was in the lowest gear, the granny ring reserved for the steepest inclines. Her face was steeled in grim determination.

The evening before, as we made camp in the rain under a stand of oak brush at the foot of Wolf Creek Pass, she'd voiced serious reservations about making it all the way to the top. She was tired, she said. She was sore. "And the grade is so steep!" More to the point, she'd been harbouring a secret since Pueblo. "I once had a ... how should I say it ... a medical situation at the top of Wolf Creek."

I was trying to get a fire going using pages torn from Charles Bukowski's *Burning In Water, Drowning In Flame*. "Medical situation?" I repeated, hunching over the crumpled poetry and striking a match. *A 340 Dollar Horse and a Hundred Dollar Whore* sprang to life, lighting up the surrounding greenery that glistened and flapped in the wetness.

April described how she'd once required emergency oxygen going over the pass in a bus. She looked miserable as she sat there, legs pulled up to her chest, chin on her knees. Earlier in the day, making our way up the San Luis Valley from Alamosa, she'd complained of a crushing migraine. Once a month her head felt like it was being clove in two with a blunt axe, she said. To make matters worse, we'd forgotten to bring Vaseline to ease the inevitable saddle sores. The stopgap, a section of foam bedroll cut to the shape of her saddle, was little better than useless.

"Didn't you tick the little box on the disclaimer," I teased, "stating no to a history of respiratory ailments?"

April's hangdog expression only deepened.

"Just giving you crap." I laughed. "We'll be going a lot slower than a bus, and we can take as many breaks as we like. You'll have plenty of time to acclimatize as we ascend."

"There is *one* other thing you should probably know."

I put down the piece of firewood I was holding. "Go on."

"I had pneumonia two years ago. My lungs filled with fluid. The doctor said they could still collapse if I overdo it."

This put a different spin on things. As the eleventh-hour confession sank in, something twigged: *That's why she's so intimidated by hills.*

I felt a twinge of irritation at only now being privy to this crucial piece of information. Scaling the Rockies was obviously a tremendous challenge for April, an opportunity to overcome her fear of altitude.

But at what price? Even if our lame-duck duo did make it to the top of the mountain, the likelihood of one or both of us being hauled away in an ambulance had suddenly increased dramatically. On the other hand, if she went home now, how would I control my descent?

SHORTLY AFTER EIGHT, sunshine splashed across our faces and the canyon walls bevelled out to sloping scree. Lodge pole pines bristled at the sky like cocktail sticks, making for breathtaking scenery.

We pulled over to take a break. "How're things, April?"

"Good, good," she giggled. "The dried prunes we had for breakfast certainly seem to be helping."

"Jet propulsion. Isn't that cheating?"

"Hey, it's still human power."

The route up and over the Continental Divide had improved dramatically since the pioneer days, back then a two-day ordeal in a Ford Model T grinding up a washed-out gravel track clinging to the mountainside. Nevertheless, I still anticipated it taking the best part of a day given our respective handicaps.

As the slope steepened, I angled my skates out even further to keep from rolling backwards. This meant taking up a wider swath of road, perilous if it weren't for the merciful reappearance of a hard shoulder. It was the 4th of July weekend, an excuse for Americans to celebrate their independence from King George III by guzzling large quantities of weak beer. The road was thick with holiday traffic: SUVs towing trailers loaded with four-wheelers, one-tonne dually pickups groaning with camping gear, and huge lumbering RVs, the terrifying sort with names like *Wilderness Intruder* and *Komfort King*, driven by bone-headed drivers oblivious to the length or width of their vehicles.

Two miles from the summit, six hours into the climb, we stopped again to rest. The air at 10,000 feet was noticeably thinner. April slumped over her handlebars and let her head loll. She looked as beat as I felt.

"What do you reckon, Ms A," I wheezed. "Time to call in the meat wagon?"

She just shook her head, chest rising and falling in quick, shallow bursts. *God, doesn't this woman EVER bitch and moan?* I thought. Ten minutes went by. "Okay," she whispered, taking a pull from her purple water bottle. "Let's go get this mountain."

Spurred on by the all-American sound bite, we picked up speed through an avalanche tunnel, ears reverberating with the roar of engines, and re-emerged into blinding sunlight. High mountain meadows teeming with white daisies and blue and mauve wild flowers crowded in on all sides. A cluster of ski resort buildings took shape, underlining patches of residual snow clinging to the slopes beyond. Another switchback, another hundred-foot jump in elevation, then the top of the pass finally appeared, announced by a large, orange sign.

April brought her bike to a stop with a wheel either side of the Great Divide, so-named for splitting North America down the middle—rain falling to the east drained into the Atlantic, to the west into the Pacific.

"I did it," she beamed, raising her fists in triumph.

"You certainly did, April. Fantastic effort!"

"And you ... know what?" She panted between breaths. "I think this was ... harder than ... being in ... labour."

AFTER SNAPPING A photo in front of the tourist sign, we readied ourselves for the twenty-four-mile descent into Pagosa Springs. I sat down on the kerb to tighten my skates. When I stood up and turned to go, April was nowhere to be seen.

I caught up with her three miles down the mountain. She was admiring the view at a lookout point, munching happily on a doughnut.

Her face fell at the sight of my dusty hair and bloodied torso. Having dragged my right boot in a t-stop for the first mile, I'd eventually picked up too much speed and had to bail off into the deep gravel of a runaway truck ramp.

"Forget something?" I asked angrily.

"Oh jeez. I'm so, so sorry."

"What the hell happened?"

"I guess I—I just got carried away. Going downhill felt so good. I completely forgot what I was here to do. I mean, that's why you had me along, right?"

"That was the idea."

"So, does this mean I'm fired?"

There was nothing to fire her from, of course. She was the one doing me a favour.

"Don't worry about it," I replied, temper subsiding. "My leg muscles are starting to feel a bit stronger. I should be able to carry my backpack once we reach Pagosa. Then you can catch the bus back to Pueblo."

She winced at the words.

I'd suspected for some time that April was smitten with heading west, following in the footsteps of the early pioneers, legendary mountain men like Jedediah Smith, Jim Bridger, and the explorers Lewis and Clarke. She'd had a taste of life on the road as a frontierswoman, blazing a trail into the real, untamed America arching all the way to the Pacific—sleeping under the stars, listening to the coyotes howl in the vast emptiness. Even with the cold, the rain, the saddle sores, and the grouchy travelling companion, she was hungry for more.

"You'd like to carry on, wouldn't you?" I said quietly.

She nodded slowly.

"But what about ..."

"Responsibilities?"

"Well, yeah."

She sighed. "You know what, Jason? I've been responsible all my life. Always followed the rules. Always gone along sedately with the rest of the herd. But like Thelma and Louise said, 'I've had it up to my ass with sedate'." She smiled and glanced away. "Oh, I know I'm being selfish, but … I just need this one thing, this one time, for me. To learn how to breathe again. To live the dream."

"But it'll be hell going through the desert," I countered. "There'll be rattlesnakes and scorpions and dust storms. And what if we run out of water? Besides, I can be a Grade A asshole, remember. What happens if …"

April wasn't listening anymore. She was gazing misty-eyed at the valley rolling out before us, its verdant pastures dotted with fat lazy cattle, gambrel barns, and the San Juan river looping off into the haze, stringing together a series of glittering lakes like jewels on a necklace. She was already out there, riding the Mother Road, the old Route 66 she'd always dreamed of one day taking.

IN PAGOSA SPRINGS, a passing police car barked at me through the bullhorn to *"Remove the skates and get off the road now!"* I took them off and started walking, then slipped them back on as soon as the cop was out of sight. An hour later, at the top of a two-mile grade heading towards Durango, the same patrol car appeared coming from the opposite direction. This time the state trooper stopped and wrote out a fine for $17. "Next time it'll be jail, mister," he warned. "The lady can ride, but you gotta walk."

Spirits dampened, we trudged back into town, April pushing her bike. To relieve aching muscles and review our options (walking all the way to San Francisco clearly wasn't one of them), we asked directions to the hot mineral springs for a soak.

It was dark by the time we found the place. In the parking lot outside we bumped into Jerry Knox, a wrangler from Missouri we'd met on the east side of Wolf Creek Pass. With his ten-gallon hat, lumberjack shirt, and ginger beard, Jerry looked like he'd just walked out of a Louis L'Amour novel. He was on his way to the Grand Canyon, he said, to take up seasonal work as a mule handler. We invited him to join us.

"Ah dunno," he said gruffly. "This place smells real bad."

April laughed. "It's the sulphur in the hot springs, Jerry."

"And we're fixin' to get in it?"

Jerry spoke slowly and deliberately, like the Cheyenne Arapahos I'd met at the Canton Lake Pow-wow in Oklahoma, and the ranchers around Rye, Colorado. The farther west you go in America, the harder the land and the harder the people. It shows in the way they talk, as frugal with words as they are with their ways.

Using the serrated edge of his hunting knife, Jerry proceeded to hack off his jeans above the knees. "Just conformin' to dress code," he explained. "Don't wanna offend nobody."

"They'll make a very nice pair of swimming trunks once they're done," April remarked. "Maybe even spark a new fashion trend?"

"Ya never know," agreed Jerry. "Wait till you see my white legs. Ya'll won't be in the dark very long."

Next morning, April and I were no closer to a solution. We sat reeking of rotten eggs in the Junction Family Dining Restaurant, drinking complimentary coffee refills and mulling over how I could leave the state of Colorado without being arrested and thrown in jail.

Halfway through her third cup, April hit upon an idea. "I have a cunning plan," she said, grabbing a handful of quarters and hurrying outside to the pay phone. Twenty minutes later she was back with tremendous news. Half a dozen calls to as many government agencies had led her to the state governor's office in Denver.

"I told the governor's assistant about your accident. She said the least Colorado could do after breaking your legs and delaying the expedition for so long was to let you leave."

Once a copy of my passport and supporting letter from UNESCO was faxed through, the governor would grant me permission to exit the state on inline skates via a less-trafficked road.

April smiled wryly. "I immediately called the Pagosa Springs Police Department to notify them of the special permit to the New Mexico border. They weren't best pleased to have the rug pulled out from underneath them, and by a politician at that!"

OUR PRESCRIBED PASSAGE took us south towards Chama on State Road 84. Four hours of uphill slog on another bollock-ache, band-aid surface, and the state line came into sight. *About to leave Colorful Colorado*, the sign read, *Mountains and Much More*. The scenery meanwhile had undergone a dramatic transformation: jagged peaks softening to kinder, more undulating high-country terrain interlaced with tabletop mesa bluffs. To the north, saucer-shaped splinters of ebony cloud hovered UFO-like above the horizon, underscoring giant cloud clusters mushrooming into the troposphere as if spewed from the mouths of smouldering volcanoes.

April had also undergone a transformation, the result of spotting a sports shop on our way out of Pagosa. Decked out in Lycra bike shorts, black sports bra, and a black Camelbak, she now had the sleek, sophisticated look of an Ironman triathlete.

We turned west towards Farmington, following a winding gorge filled with sagebrush and pine. Abandoned homesteads littered the scrubby surrounds, grave markers to the cindered dreams of settlers who'd once broken their backs here—working the land, busting sod, ploughing their lifesavings into a harsh, merciless landscape, itself knowing nothing of charity from the elements that fashioned it.

By eight o'clock, well past sundown, our legs were tired and our throats screaming. We'd stayed out on the road longer in the hope of finding a petrol station or roadside store selling cold beer. When a sign informed us we were crossing into the Jicarilla Apache Nation, all hope faded. Sale of alcohol was prohibited on the majority of Indian reservations countrywide. We started looking for somewhere to pull off the road and camp. Then, like the rising Star of Bethlehem, the tatty yellow neon of the Gomez Bar loomed in the western sky.

"That," I said, "is a sight for sore thighs."

Parking the bike outside, we entered a tin shed stinking of disinfectant, comprising of a liquor store at one end, a toilet at the other, and a pair of decrepit pool tables in the middle. Sinister ne'er-do-wells slouched over the bar swilling bottles of Miller High Life and yakking drunkenly over the jukebox. Under the steady gaze of every eyeball in the house, April and I made our way to the bar and ordered a couple. Then a couple more—the day had been long and blisteringly hot. A character looking harder than a box of concrete lurched towards us, pool cue in hand. His black, lanky hair was barely restrained by a knotted bandana, and his death's head sweatshirt was torn at the shoulder, exposing the tattoo of a bird-eating spider.

Bloody hell, I thought, adrenaline pumping. *Here we fucking go!*

"Les Howland." He offered his free hand. "Would you and your lady friend like to play me and my brother Scott?"

Regaining my composure, I managed to choke out, "Sure, what are we playing for?" fully expecting the answer to be: "Your lady friend."

"Round of beer?"

"Sounds good."

They were the resident pool sharks, sensing easy prey. April cued off, the picture of virtue in her white tee shirt, white socks, and white cap. It was Wendy Darling versus the villainous pirate, Captain Hook. But the brothers were obviously having an off night. Two hours and five beers later, April and I found ourselves leading four games to three, an unprecedented upheaval in the Jicarilla Apache Nation cosmos.

"So, where're you guys stayin' tonight?" asked Scott, making small talk between shots.

"We'll just lay our sleeping bags out back," I replied.

"Careful. There's a ladda broken glass out there."

The Howlands thrashed us the next three games and invited us to stay in their mobile home. Allowing no time for an answer, Les tossed April's bike on the roof of his jalopy and pulled around to the drive-through. "Get in," he ordered. "I wanna introduce you guys to someone."

The sales attendant, possibly old Gomez himself, frowned from his booth and shook his head. *"Be careful,"* he mouthed as the brothers loaded a crate of beer in the back. Obviously, he knew something we didn't. Did the brothers have rap sheets longer than their pool cues? Had other weary travellers partaken of their hospitality, only to vanish and never be heard of again?

Or perhaps he was trying to warn us of the foot-long rat living in Les's trailer. While the four of us sat on the floor, drinking beer and jamming—Les on guitar, me on harmonica—Houdini the rat scuttled back and forth, disappearing, reappearing, then disappearing again.

"That's why I call him Houdini." Les grinned happily.

April clapped her hands with delight as the rodent galloped across her lap for the umpteenth time. "Ooh, how adorable!"

"Yeah, cute little fella isn't he," I said coolly, suppressing the urge to ask if it was really the same rat that kept appearing. *Doubtless this place is stiff with vermin,* I thought to myself. *Home to an entire menagerie of Houdinis.*

WITH ITS BELLIGERENT drivers, filthy oil and gas activity, and car lot after car lot of testosterone-packing pickup trucks, we couldn't get through Farmington quick enough. Why would anyone want to live in such a hellish place, I wondered? Flaking mobile homes stood orphaned in the heat, permeating the air with the constant hum of air conditioning. I glimpsed a young girl through the diamond pattern of a chain-link fence, her complexion the deep, dusky ochre of the surrounding Entrada limestone, contrasting sharply against a clothesline sagging with white bed linen. For a moment, I caught her eye. Bored, disaffected, and resigned, her vacant gaze said it all.

But if there is a fault to travel, it is the idle presumption of summing up places on the fly. On the west side of town, a beat-up station wagon slowed alongside April, who was looking tired and fed up. The window rolled down and an old Navajo woman waved a gnarled fist in friendly solidarity. "Go, road warrior," she rasped. "You can make it." Then the car sped away, leaving us humbled and our hasty impression of Farmington overruled.

We pushed on to Teec Nos Pos, a dusty intersection marking the four corners of Colorado, New Mexico, Arizona, and Utah. The landscape became prehistoric and interesting again. To the south, the twin-bladed monolith of Shiprock broke the skyline, piercing the planetary crust like a splintered sword. To the north, brownie-shaped slabs of geology teetered over a barren plain creased into gentle folds by time. We were now entering the desolate badlands of the Navajo Nation.

After a few miles we took a breather against a steel crash barrier. A white Chevrolet van pulled in behind us.

"We was just readin' about you guys."

A middle-aged Navajo man holding a newspaper ambled over to shake our hands. The previous morning, we'd stopped in town long enough to be interviewed. The result was a surprisingly flattering full-page article in *The Farmington Daily News*.

The man, whose name was Charley, tapped the paper hopefully. "We was wonerin' if you might autograph it."

April fished for a pen. "Who would you like it signed to?"

"To the Interpreter family. As in translators."[*]

While April scribbled a note, I made the usual small talk: "Where are you guys coming from?"

"Kayenta. We was takin' our kids to a movie out in Farmington."

April looked up. "How much farther is Teec?"

"Oh, it's just right there." Charley turned and pointed. "You go over the state line, about another eight miles."

This was welcome news. The day was a scorcher. Perhaps we'd find some shade there.

"Well, good luck." Charley started back to his van.

"Hey, hold up." April hurried after him. "Let me get your mailing address." She'd have a complimentary world map sent from Rand Mc-Nally, she explained, for the kids to follow the expedition on their classroom wall. Although still in its infancy, the World Wide Web allowed Nancy to make periodic updates to our fledgling website.

Before taking off, Charley jogged back with a $10 bill in his hand. "Somethin' for your trip," he said.

April looked flustered. "Oh—no, no."

"Go on, take it." Charley pushed the note towards her. "Buy you guys a meal or somethin'."

Watching the van disappear, I turned to April and said, "You know, we should spend the next couple of days riding up and down this stretch of road. Cash in while the story's hot."

April, nibbling on an oatmeal bar, erupted with choking laughter, sending a nugget of cereal flying. "I didn't know whether to take his money or not!"

---

[*]   Charley's grandfather had been an interpreter for the US Army and adopted the name.

"Well, it's okay if a person is right there in front of you, so you can look them in the eye."

"As you take their money?"

"Yeah. Then leave them bound and gagged by the side of the road."

"While you make off with their truck."

Most Americans in my experience didn't care for this form of malignant humour, preferring more overt in-your-face comedy. Yet, here was sweet, mild-mannered April, American to the tip of her Colorado Rockies baseball cap, putting the boot in like the most sick-humoured Brit.

The state sign declared that Arizona was THE HOT STATE, but there was no mention of the wind, a relentless bullying thing that roared in our ears and clawed at our skin. It was dead on the nose, too, doing its level best to shove us back into New Mexico, undeterred by the low-lying salt brush and smattering of piñons. The road dipped and rose like a giant roller coaster unfurling itself at tortuous half-mile increments, blacktop glistening in the afternoon sun, false peaks leading on and on into blistering haze.

Eight miles from the Red Mesa Trading Post, I caught up with April who'd ground to a halt with her head on her forearms.

"Can we see the sea yet?" she wailed at her feet.

I looked up and saw that there was indeed a sea, a sea of shimmering crests stretching to the horizon, a cruel illusion we'd be chasing all the way to the Pacific. For the next 600 miles, until the Sierras, it was nothing but desert.

"We're almost there," I lied. "Another couple of miles to Red Mesa. Try not to look at your bike computer. It'll only depress you."

It was three in the afternoon, the hottest time of the day. Our surroundings afforded no shade, and our body temperatures were steadily climbing. The only option was to push on before one of us succumbed to heatstroke, the most common cause of death for hundreds of illegal immigrants crossing the Arizona desert from Mexico each year.*

A little later, in another bid to boost morale, I said, "I think I can see the legs of a water tower up ahead. That's got to be it."

April squinted into the glare. "Hmm, I'm not seeing it."

"Well, just imagine it's there for now."

Barely managing a walking pace, we finally reached the Trading Post and spent the next thirty minutes sipping ice water in the air conditioning, our eyes closed, saying nothing. It was another soulless roadside joint—naked cinderblocks, bars on the windows, fluorescent lights, and the gagging aroma of sweet buttered popcorn and stale coffee—but to us it was an oasis of life.

The next day was the same: blast furnace heat by ten, and a screaming headwind every inch of the way. According to the map, we were now tracing the northern edge of the Painted Desert, a gnawed carcass of ivory whites and bloodless pinks picked clean by millennia of wind and water. Five cyclists in garish Lycra came hurtling out of the west, the wind at their backs. Faces steeled in concentration, eyes glued to the tarmac, the Race Across America contestants never even saw us.† But this was typical of endurance riders. Saint Peter could have been dancing the fandango in a leotard and they wouldn't have noticed.

West of Kayenta, my skate wheels became bogged in patches of molten tar and the smell of grilled chicken filled the air. When your skin starts to sizzle, you know it's time to get out of the sun.

Ting-ting-ting-ting.

---

* According to the United States Border Patrol, 2,190 people died crossing the US–Mexico border between 1996 and 2004. Caused by failure of the body's temperature-regulating mechanism when exposed to excessively high temperatures, heatstroke is a condition marked by fever, unconsciousness, and eventually death.

† Race Across America (RAAM) is an ultra-endurance bicycle race across the US. There are no stages or rest periods. The fastest riders typically complete the 3,000-mile course in 8-9 days.

I looked at April. "Am I imagining that?"

"Bells. Yes, I'm hearing them too."

We traced the sound to a culvert under the road, a square concrete tunnel built for flash floods spilling off the impenetrable terrain. Miniature sand dunes fluted by the wind ran the length of the interior, and coarse Navajo graffiti etched in charcoal prettified the walls. At the far end, the silhouetted forms of a dozen sheep lay panting. One had a bell around its neck.

Ting-ting-ting-ting

"Mind if we get a little shade, too?" I hollered.

A low growl echoed from the darkness. A dog!

"Please," April begged, tiptoeing closer. "We'll just sit at this end. That way we can all rest."

I thought of the swan house on Madeira, the torrential rainstorm, and how I'd evicted the residents without compunction. Now we were in a similar predicament, only with the outside temperature well over a hundred degrees instead of rain. Maybe it was the smell of barbecued meat that did it. Suddenly the entire entourage, canine chaperone included, clambered to its feet and shuffled out the other side.

I felt guilty. For about two seconds. The flood tunnel was like crawling into a fridge—deliciously cold. Sitting with our backs against the cool concrete, our core temperatures quickly stabilized. I closed my eyes and pictured a very different confrontation our cave-dwelling ancestors might have faced competing for shelter against a far deadlier adversary.

When I awoke, it was to the ringing of bells.

Ting-ting-ting-ting

The herd was trooping back, two by two, like Noah's little four-foot starter colony. The direct sun was too much for them. Flopping back down in the shade, they resumed chewing the cud.

Ting-ting-ting-ting

After a few minutes April had the bridge of her nose pinched between thumb and forefinger, like she did during one of her migraines.

"That noise is starting to get really obnoxious," I murmured.

The sound of yet more bells approached, these with more of a *clang* to them than *ting*. Two-dozen longhaired goats with beautiful twisting horns marched in, half of them wearing bells. The effect was a veritable cacophony, a band of cloven-hoofed Quasimodos turned loose with the contents of the kitchen sink.

Ting-CLANG-Ting-CLANG-Ting-CLANG-Ting-CLANG.

We threw our sandals. We shouted. I even played my harmonica, normally guaranteed to put any living thing to flight. It was no use. Jamming our fingers in our ears, we retreated into the scorching heat, heavenly respite in comparison.

THE CALIFORNIA DESERT
RIDING THE MOTHER ROAD

If daisies are your favorite flower, keep pushing up that engine power.

—BURMA-SHAVE ROAD SIGN, ROUTE 66

EYOND FLAGSTAFF, EVERYTHING STARTED funnelling west like a giant tube of toothpaste squeezing towards the Pacific: power lines, the Santa Fe Railway, and historic Route 66, which we joined at Williams. Once the poster child of a golden age of motoring—*"If you ever plan to motor west, travel my way, the highway that's the best. Get your kicks on Route 66!"**—the Mother Road was now little more than an aide-mémoire crumbling in the wake of Dwight D. Eisenhower's post-war Interstate Highway System. Grass grew liberally from fissures wide enough to swallow my skate wheels, and rattling ghost towns emerged from the windswept plain, the few surviving stores and restaurants hanging on selling pricey memorabilia and shoddy food to a captive trickle of sentimentalists.

April, a hopeless romantic herself, was unfazed by the deterioration: "This is *so* cool!"

We rode into Ashfork as dusk was falling. Clapped-out motels and gas stations stood frozen in the 1950s. Dogs lunged against chain link fences, and kids on trick bikes zigzagged between faded lines in the road, pulling wheelies. Hank Williams floated from The Crow Bar on Main Street, red neon blinking in the semi-darkness.

"This is it, Jason. Hometown America. Just like when I was a kid."

We made camp in an alfalfa field on the edge of town and cooked a typical evening meal: stir-fried mushrooms, peppers, ginger root, garlic, and boiled rice, followed by s'mores washed down with sweetened black tea.†

The heat index continued to soar as we clocked our highest mileage, ninety-eight miles, coasting on the satin-smooth Interstate 40 (somehow we'd lost the 66 heading out of Kingman) down to the Colorado River. The following day in Needles, California, the temperature nudged 124 degrees.

---

*   Bobby Troup.
†   An American campfire favourite, s'mores are a deliciously gooey amalgam of Graham crackers, chocolate, and melted marshmallows.

"Now that's hot!" April exclaimed, grimacing at the digital thermometer above the town hall.

If the Arizona fuzz had turned a blind eye to a cyclist and rollerblader using the motorway, the California Highway Patrol (CHP), the same chiselled heroes from the 1970s cop series *CHiPs* I'd watched as a kid, made it their business to harass us from the get-go. Ten miles west of Needles, we were unceremoniously booted off the I-40 and back onto the old road, now in such an advanced state of disrepair it could hardly be described as one.

"Hope we've brought enough water," I said to April as we slogged up the modest if seemingly never-ending incline towards Barstow, one hundred and fifty cerebrum-melting miles through the Mojave Desert. The combination of uphill and appalling surface meant we were averaging less than six miles per hour.

In a bid to preserve the moisture in her mouth, my travelling partner merely nodded in reply.

Back in Needles, thinking we could resupply at service stations and rest areas along the main highway, we'd opted to save weight by filling only the Camelbak and three half-litre bottles. This, I now realized, was a big mistake. On the unplanned-for old road, with its fractured surface snaking off into a shimmering puddle of heat, there was no way of knowing where the next water stop would be.

In two hours not a single vehicle passed. By three o'clock, April had just a few mouthfuls left in her Camelbak. We stopped beside a low trestle bridge that supported the railway running parallel to the road. Beneath the tar-coated sleeper ties, there was just enough room for us to wriggle in out of the heat. April took off her baseball cap and let her body go limp against the cold alluvial sand.

"Feels heavenly." She shivered with pleasure.

It was no more than a bolthole from the sun, buying us a little time to work out what to do next. I drifted off, waking with a start to a terrifying sound, a great rumbling through the desert like an approaching army. Before either of us could slither out from our reptilian lair, the freight train was upon us, boxcars squealing and grinding in our faces, timbers bowing alarmingly and sending down a light drizzle of sand. Then the last car clattered past, and the jostling steel receded into the east.

I glanced at April. "You okay?"

Her eyes were wide like saucers. "Got a little Western there for a minute." She laughed nervously. "I've always found trains quite, um … intimidating."

As the afternoon wore on, the dull, bludgeoning heat gave way to a more tolerable ferocity. The sensible option, we decided, was to backtrack to Needles and try again at first light. With Barstow three or more days away, we needed to carry as much water as possible.

I was out on the road buckling down my skates when a white pickup pulled up, the first vehicle we'd seen since I-40. A Union Pacific decal caught my eye. Railroad engineers. The window slid down, releasing a heavenly wave of air conditioning. It was all I could do not to thrust my head inside.

"Evrithin' awright?" asked the bewhiskered driver.

April smiled sweetly. "Actually, we've run a little low on water." This was an understatement. We'd run out completely. "You wouldn't happen to have any extra would you?"

The engineer reached around to a cooler and pulled out a fistful of ice-cold bottles. I handed one to April and screwed the top off another. That first trickle down my throat was like stepping into Woody Allen's "orgasmatron." April's dazed expression suggested she was experiencing something similar.

Reinvigorated and with bottles to spare, we thanked our Good Samaritans and reverted to the original plan. The mining town of Goffs was only ten miles away, they said. We could fill up our water bottles there.

It was dusk by the time we arrived. The place was deserted: no service stations, no shops, no outside taps. If Goffs had a pulse, it was undetectable. The horse had either died or galloped off a long time ago. The town now played host to a collection of rotten shacks, depressed-looking cacti, and a creaking windmill that hadn't pumped water in half a century, by the look of it.

At the centre of town, the road split. The right fork took off north towards the Soda Mountains, a dark, foreboding mass brooding against the evening sky. The left veered back towards the highway, visible in the half-light as a procession of winking headlamps migrating slowly through the desert. Either we continued to roll loaded dice in a waterless hellhole of heat, wind, and flyblown ghost towns, or face the Boys in Blue on I-40. If we managed to bluff our way, the latter offered a smooth, serviced road all the way to Barstow.

I turned to April. "So, what do you reckon, Thelma?"

The schoolteacher gazed into the orange glow of the western desert and let out a heavy sigh. "Well, I can tell you one thing. I've had it up to my ass with old Route 66."

"YOU'LL HAVE TO leave the interstate at the next exit," drawled the CHP officer, who, down to his testicle-hugging trousers, bore more than a passing resemblance to Officer Frank Poncherello. The policeman slid into his spiel about how dangerous it was for us to be on the highway, one I guessed from his insouciant expression he'd given to legions of transcontinental cyclists, skateboarders, pogo stick devotees, and all manner of Forrest Gump wannabes over the years.

April and I just stood there, looking suitably contrite. Our rehearsed response, when it came, was to inform "Ponch" of a special permit arranged through the California State Governor's office in Sacramento.

"We called their office yesterday," I said matter-of-factly. "They said they'd have it faxed through to the nearest highway patrol station. Didn't your office receive it yet?"

Ponch replied that no, his office hadn't, which wasn't altogether surprising seeing as a permit hadn't been applied for in the first place.

"Well, that's strange." April feigned surprise. "Mind you, the governor's office doesn't open until nine. Maybe it'll come through in the next few hours."

It was 7:40 am. Ponch sniffed, stalked back to his car, and sped away. Our whopping fib had bought us some extra time.

Not much, as it turned out. Two hours later he was back, this time looking agitated.

"This permit," he snapped, "still hasn't come through."

The game was up. Off we went in single file, cars beeping jeeringly as they passed. I cursed our luck. Back on the rotten old 66, provisioned with only two litres of drinking water, carrying on to Barstow would be madness. Then again, retracing our steps to Needles without succumbing to dehydration wouldn't be easy, either.

Fate, however, was about to intercede on our behalf. As we neared the off-ramp, the patrol car went *"Whoop!"* and took off in a flurry of flashing lights. An all stations alert had won us another temporary reprieve.

Ignoring Ponch's instructions, April and I made it another twenty unmolested miles to the safe haven of Ludlow, a collection of petrol pumps and pop machines in the middle of the desert. An orange work vest donated by a resurfacing crew smoothed the final fifty-mile dash to Barstow, the high-visibility material lending an air of sufficient officialdom to bamboozle the two patrol cars that passed.

The first person we met was the mayor. She was having lunch in Taco Bell, the Mexican fast food chain known for being cheaper than cat food.

"So what do you guys think of Barstow?" she asked.

The short amount of time April and I had spent inside the city limits suggested it comprised of soulless vehicle dealerships sandwiched between roachy motels and greasy taco joints. But, as our recent experience in Farmington had taught us, first impressions nearly always turn out to be misguided.

"It's wonderful," I replied. And I meant it. The interstate highway and the worst of the desert were behind us. Our destination, San Francisco, felt almost tangible.

SLEEPING BAGS SWINGING from the handlebars, enamel cups clinking and other accoutrements bouncing against the panniers, April's rig looked quite different to how it had started out five weeks before in Colorado. The person riding it looked very different, too. Arms copper-toned, legs tempered to steel, and an easy assuredness that comes with experience, April was now a pro as we entered John Steinbeck's fabled San Joaquin Valley.

The evening before, having shouldered into an unremitting westerly all the way from Barstow, we'd reached the sprawling town of Mojave at the foot of the Sierra Nevada. Even the Joshua trees leaned in deference to the wind. Pushing on in the predawn cool to the top of Tehachapi Pass, crowned by its bristling forest of wind turbines, we'd swept down the other side through hills sculpted like butterballs, eventually levelling out to a chequerboard maze of geometric squares tinged a thousand shades of green.

Roads and windbreaks zigzagged the valley floor with cookie-cutter ease, unravelling far into the humidified haze. We entered the migrant realm by way of Arvin, an agricultural backwater filled with scowling Hispanics, and "the air so heavy with irrigation," April remarked, "you'd have to be an amphibian to live here."

On we spun over gloriously smooth surfaces to Buttonwillow, past lavish vineyards and fields of cotton, tomatoes, garlic, and citrus, and rambling machine yards festooned with tangled heaps of irrigation pipe. Road-kill veggies abounded, squeezed into our panniers and dominating evening stews. Sporadic herds of nodding donkeys greeted us, bowing blindly at the Earth in messianic devotion to the black gold hidden beneath. Then it was over one last range of hills to Santa Cruz, pulling out all the stops in the failing light. Gaily painted beach shacks gave way to sandstone cliffs flushed by the delicate pinks of the gloaming. And finally there it was, fanning out before us in all its glory: The mighty Pacific.

But our journey wasn't over quite yet.

7:54 pm. September 1, 1996. Fifty miles south of San Francisco

"I RECKON THIS is our best campsite yet," April murmured.

I nodded, staring out to sea. "Yup. Certainly a hard one to beat."

"Best of all it doesn't cost a dime."

We were sitting out of the wind in a dip hollowed from the cliff, a carpet of spongy-leaved ice plant cushioning our aching frames. Seabirds looped and wheeled in the updraft above us. In the middle distance, the onshore breeze sucked and pawed at the Pacific, mauling its surface into legions of white horses. Farther still, tapering to the horizon, a luminous wedge shone like a mirror: the sun cavorting in its own image.

Truly, we were kings! Blessed with a small corner of the planet we could call home—for a few hours at least—we didn't owe anyone a thing. No fees. No taxes. No rules. In a world gone money-grubbing mad with the invention of ownership and extracting every last penny for personal gain, such sanctuaries were hard to come by.

April was watching a V-shaped squadron of pelicans tracking northwards, their stubby wings meting out their faithful stroke, making it all look so easy. "This is *freedom!*" she cried out suddenly.

It wasn't mere hyperbole. School started in a few days. Her grand adventure was drawing to a close.

"And our journey's end," I noted soberly, picking up a loose stone and lobbing it into the thrashing surf below.

Feeling somewhat ambivalent about the imminent completion, we both fell silent. Setting out from Pueblo seven weeks earlier, I'd fully expected one of us to quit on the first day—most likely me with my left tibia not healed properly. But, as the days rolled into weeks, the shooting pains had subsided as the muscles regained their former strength, and now I was about to become the first person to inline skate across the US. *No mean feat for someone who's never rollerbladed before,* I reflected. On the flip side, it would be another penniless arrival in another honking metropolis, sponsorship as elusive as ever. How many months of soul-destroying fundraising would it take to move the expedition forward this time?

Next day we knocked out the remaining fifty-five miles to the northernmost tip of the San Francisco Peninsula: up Cabrillo Highway to Point Lobos Avenue, past the Cliff House, then through the maze of the demilitarized Presidio. Twilight was creeping in as we brought our wheels to a halt beside the rufous red towers of the Golden Gate Bridge.

A strolling couple offered to snap our picture. "Unbelievable!" the woman exclaimed after hearing April's story. She was in her mid-twenties and of Chinese descent. She looked at the teacher in silent wonderment. "You did this? Did you know how long it was going to take?"

April looked shyly at her feet. "No. I just … did it. I wanted to tell my kids what it was like to be on an expedition first-hand."

Feeling like a proud parent, I cut in: "And she'd never ridden a bicycle more than a few miles before setting out."

"Oh my God. Incredible. Did you stay in hotels?"

I thought of Houdini the rat scuttling over our slumbering bodies in Les Howland's trailer in New Mexico. "No, we've got sleeping bags. Most nights we just rolled them out by the side of the road."

"I can't believe this!"

The couple wandered off, shaking their heads and whispering, leaving April and me to muse on our journey's end. Twinkling streetlights sputtered to life in the East Bay. The moon, heavy and crimson, levered herself over the eastern lip of the world, even as a lone foghorn boomed through the darkness, a dull, mournful chant that tugged at my heart like the freight trains in Alabama and Mississippi. My thoughts turned to the people I'd met along the way, all those good Americans who'd taken me in and fed me, sheltered me, scraped me off the side of the road and fixed me up again, sending me off with emphatic goodwill ringing in my ears, westwards in the footsteps of their great-grandparents. I imagined them all sleeping soundly under the same blood-red moon stretching all the way to the Atlantic, thousands of miles across the gravid bulge of that darkening continent. And as I stood there, reflecting on how lucky I was to be alive at this, the farthest edge of the Western world, the fog came in, a great waxen shroud sweeping low across the Pacific, boiling under the bridge and scaling the cliffs of the South Bay, before enveloping us like a soundless assassin.

San Francisco
The Seed Buried Deep

I have found out that there ain't no surer way to find out whether you
like people or hate them than to travel with them.

—Mark Twain, *Tom Sawyer Abroad*

S TEVE AND EILBHE HAD arrived in San Francisco seven months earlier. Starting with a phone number of a friend of a friend scribbled on a napkin in a New Orleans coffee shop, they'd networked and couch-surfed their way across the city. Eilbhe tailored hats, sweaters, and scarves to make ends meet, selling her wares at local flea markets. Steve spoke at luncheon club meetings and took whatever under-the-table work he could find, from nude modelling to working a concession on one of the ferries to Alcatraz Island.

I caught up with them on a rented yacht, *Aqui No Mas,* in the Fisherman's Wharf district. Seeing that living space was tight, I took my chances in nearby Fort Mason Park. Sleeping rough in a big city was a very different undertaking to camping on the open road, and San Francisco had its own set of peculiarities. The couple in the next bush over turned out to be homosexual methamphetamine addicts who spent their days panhandling the tourist district of North Beach and their nights quarrelling over domestic issues. Voices would be raised. Fists would fly. Eventually, differences resolved, they'd make up like any loving couple by having loud rambunctious sex—an all-out buggery in a shrubbery.

Moksha was also in town. At a talk I'd given earlier in the year at the Colorado State University in Pueblo, one of the audience members, an engineering student, had volunteered the use of his car, a hulking great thing with a V8 engine powerful enough to tow *Moksha* across the country. Kenny drove "The Behemoth" the first leg from Fort Lauderdale to Colorado. The onward leg to the West Coast offered a chance to extend an olive branch to Chris Tipper, still aggrieved at his treatment by Steve two and a half years earlier. Doctor Ken sponsored a ticket, and Chris helped me tow *Moksha* the rest of the way to San Francisco, carving out a little holiday for himself in the process. He also agreed to make the boat seaworthy for the Pacific. The centreboard casing was still cracked from running aground on the reef outside Providenciales, and the rudder more recently damaged after being rear-ended en route to a school presentation in Colorado Springs.

But lasting reconciliation with the shipwright was not to be. A misunderstanding over use of tools at *Moksha's* new home, the maritime museum at Hyde Street Pier, led to the boat being impounded and ransomed for $250. Steve was furious. Regardless of the circumstances, Chris and I were ultimately to blame, once again leaving the boat builder feeling snubbed and humiliated. He returned to England vowing to have nothing to do with the expedition ever again.

To be fair, finding affordable quarters for a 26-foot-long pedal boat in San Francisco wasn't easy. Rejection followed rejection from boatyards and yacht clubs alike. The secretary of the prestigious Saint Francis Yacht Club took one look at *Moksha's* dilapidated appearance (she'd been mouldering under a tarpaulin in Fort Lauderdale for over a year) and showed us the door. In the end, however, these rebuffs were a blessing in disguise, for they led in a roundabout way to the infinitely superior camaraderie offered by the Delta House of all boating establishments, the legendary Bay View Boat Club.

Starting out life on a floating barge moored in San Francisco Bay, a crafty loophole to avoid a liquor licence, the club was a renowned haunt of maverick sea captains, wily eccentrics, and semi-alcoholic miscreants up to their necks in all manner of skulduggery. *Moksha* and the expedition fitted right in. The club became our new base of operations, the American equivalent of the Guilford Street squat.

It was here that *Moksha* was acquainted with the Pacific in a touching ceremony performed by Commodore Arf Pitney, a twinkle-eyed rogue with a salt-and-pepper beard and crumbling teeth. Arf was the head kook in charge of the asylum, singularly individualistic and prone to urbane turns of phrase. Following *Moksha's* launch into China Basin, he pulled Steve and me aside and began eagerly expounding the merits of arming ourselves against would-be pirates.

"Messrs. Smith 'n Lewis," he cried, smothering us in a cloud of whiskey fumes as he pressed his florid face nearer to ours. "In the interest of deterring any unsolicited boardings, may I propose the placement of a light cannon on the foredeck of the good lady? Also, I believe it expedient to have a quantity of grapeshot on hand to fire across the bows of any ne'er-do-wells."

Grinning triumphantly, he took a moment to smooth his whiskers before launching into a spirited case for the one mode of human power he felt grossing lacking.

"Dirigibles!" He had to raise his voice above the foot-stomping reverberations of the house band, JimBo Trout and the Fishpeople, who were busy sawing and plucking their way through a blistering bluegrass set using an assortment of banjos, fiddles, and a washtub bass. "For the love of Mary and Joseph, Messrs. Smith 'n Lewis, you've crossed land and sea using your own power. Surely, a pedal-powered zeppelin over the Channel and up the Thames to finish?"

The Bay View Boat Club was also where Steve and I met to discuss the upcoming leg to Australia. It was Kenny's idea to cycle through Central and South America before tackling the Pacific. This would give us access to the same anticlockwise pattern of winds and currents that had nudged Thor Heyerdahl's balsa log raft *Kon-Tiki* to Polynesia half a century before. The alternative, beelining it from California to Queensland, faced a potentially insurmountable obstacle: a 400-mile-wide countercurrent north of the equator known as the Inter Tropical Convergence Zone, where the water flowed east at one and a half knots. Nautical experts had cast serious doubts as to whether *Moksha* could punch through to the Southern Hemisphere.

Kenny's route was duly chosen, but the detour wasn't without its own drawbacks. As well as adding 7,000 miles to the overall circumnavigation, the overland route to Peru meant hacking through a hundred miles of malaria-infested jungle between Panama and Colombia.

Contested by heavily armed militia on the payroll of rival drug cartels, the lawless Darien Gap was considered impassable to all but the most foolhardy traveller. The Trans-Americas Expedition, for example, with considerable backup from the British Army, took ninety-nine days to cross it in Range Rovers, averaging only one mile per day. Doing it on foot should take less than a quarter of that time, we calculated. Moreover, to show Her Majesty's Armed Forces up to be a bunch of girl's blouses, we decided to do it in dresses and high heels.

Overriding all these considerations was an even bigger concern, however, one I needed to share with Steve as soon as possible.

I wouldn't be pedalling the Pacific with him.

It's difficult when you know your marriage isn't working. After our stormy Atlantic crossing, I'd hoped traversing the US separately would allow us the breathing space to continue as a team. Sure enough, when Steve turned up at my bedside in Parkview Medical Center, pledging to wait it out in San Francisco until I caught up, his unshakable loyalty inspired me to wipe the slate clean. But then *Moksha* was impounded, followed by Steve's swift, dictatorial response, and the bad memories came flooding back. Had anything really changed between us, I wondered? The best of friends in settled life, maybe we just weren't cut out to be on an expedition together. The thought of being cellmates for nine months on the Pacific, three Atlantics back-to-back, was utterly mind-boggling.

"I'll bike to Alaska," I said. "Cross the Bering Straits somehow, then pedal south and meet you in Asia." We were sitting on a wooden bench in the club garden, gazing out across the ruffled water towards Oakland. "You could find another travelling partner in the meantime, someone more suitable, more of a team player. Eilbhe, perhaps?"

Steve looked stunned. I had a good idea of what was going through his head: *I've just spent seven months waiting for this bastard, and this is the thanks I get!*

"Listen, Jason," he began, "I know we've had our differences, but ..." He paused, choked with emotion. "I just can't imagine doing this trip with anyone else."

I was the traitor, the Judas, and I realized that at some point I was always going to have to make the choice between duty and freedom, obligation and truth, commitment to a fixed idea versus the fluid line of questioning Steve and I had begun at university. This was the intellectual landscape that defined our early friendship, prompting Steve to invite me on his journey in the first place and our mutual desire to see it grow as an educational tool. Except that operating within the strict, logistical parameters of an expedition, something was always going to have to give.

"Travelling with the same person can be hard," I said, trying to sound conciliatory. "It's not you, or me. It's being on the road."

This was only partly true, of course. When all was said and done, my aversion to crossing the Pacific with Steve could only really be taken personally.

"But you hate the cold, Jason. If anyone can do it, you can, but I still think travelling separately across the Pacific is a big mistake."

"I can't think of any other way, though. Can you?"

Furrowing his brow, Steve began to think. "Perhaps there's a way for us to stay a team, but get more people involved, mix things up a little. We could invite other people to pedal. Whoever's not in *Moksha* could catch a ride on a sailboat or something."

I felt goose bumps on my skin, like I had all those years ago in Paris when Steve pitched the original idea for a human-powered circumnavigation. "Okay." I nodded slowly.

"It'll be a team effort," he continued, "but still a circumnavigation. Nancy, dad, Eilbhe ... I'm sure they'd all like to have a go."

"We could even ask local folks," I added. "Women, teens, seniors. Yeah, why not!"

Steve's lateral thinking had raised the bar once again. The expedition wasn't just a line on a map. The real expedition was the seed buried deep in the heart of anyone who has ever dreamed of knowing what lies beyond their valley, and of embarking upon a grand adventure to find out. People didn't belong to the expedition. They *were* the expedition.

"Anyone can cross an ocean by human power," said Steve, his cobalt gaze reignited. "Ordinary people *can* do extraordinary things."

INSPIRED BY OUR new vision and fuelled by a fresh injection of local support, preparations for the next leg began in earnest. Seasoned corporate trainer Shirley Nice volunteered the use of her phone, fax, and computer for sending out sponsorship proposals. She also let me sleep on the living room floor of her Bernal Heights apartment, a welcome upgrade from my bush in Fort Mason Park. Most mornings we would sit out on the rear deck, surrounded by a mini-wilderness of rose bushes, flowering shrubs, and stone Buddhas meditating between towering bamboos, brainstorming and honing the expedition's educational mission. Yoga and one of Shirley's spectacular waffle and fresh fruit breakfasts would follow.

Even with keeping living expenses at a minimum, my financial situation was getting desperate. Shirley introduced me to a Guatemalan entrepreneur under contract with Disney to produce three hundred child-sized Mickey Mouses carved from wood. Could I paint their eyes and ears with black acrylic paint? For fifteen dollars an hour I reckoned I could do just about anything. But I used too much paint, which ran, of course, and by the end of the first day every Mickey Mouse was bawling its eyes out, and I was looking for a new job.

It was around this time that Shirley introduced me to Rong Rong

Zheng, a doctor skilled in the art of traditional Chinese medicine. A bone graft to properly heal my left leg was still on the cards, and I was keen to explore other healing remedies, no matter how unorthodox. The physician kindly agreed to treat me as a favour to her friend Shirley, and once a week for eight weeks I rollerbladed across town to her clinic—a cramped, unventilated room buzzing with insects. By the final visit, I knew what to expect.

"Come, England-Son!" The doctor had frizzy hair and a voice that commanded obedience. Closing the door behind me, I turned to see Rong Rong fiddling with her secret contraption, a metal shoebox marked with Chinese characters. A snarl of wires sprouted from the back, leading to an array of wicked-looking acupuncture needles. "Today we go number eight, okay?"

"That seems a bit high, Doctor."

"England-Son, you want to wake up leg or not?"

"Yes, yes, of course." I slipped off my socks and reclined on the narrow bed. "But last time we only went to number five, remember? Maybe we can go just one more notch, say, to six?"

Rong Rong was busy untangling wires and twiddling dials. Picking out a three-inch-long needle, she began working it into the muscle below my left knee, rolling it back and forth between thumb and forefinger. More followed, planted around a crater of angry red scar tissue marking the fracture site.

"Need to be strong, England-Son." The doctor shook her fists like a conquering general and set the dial to seven. "Nerves and blood vessels in leg not healing bone. Need to wake leg up!"

Before I could protest further, Rong Rong threw the master switch. My leg shot several inches into the air and hovered.

"Jesus." I winced. "That's … pretty … damn … painful."

But Doctor Zheng was not one to suffer wimps lightly. Emigrating from China in the early eighties, she'd arrived in the US equipped with only her torture device and a hundred dollars. In true American pioneer style, the indomitable physician had gone on to carve out a new life for herself, in time saving enough money to bring her husband and family over.

Ignoring my pleas, she flipped the dial to eight, elevating my leg another inch.*

As autumn turned to winter, work on *Moksha* gathered pace. The more launch-ready she was before being shipped to Peru, the fewer delays at the other end in an unknown port with unknown facilities. Her hull was painted yellow for better visibility and a slew of donated electronics installed, including anti-collision alarms, an Inmarsat-C system for email, and additional solar panels and a wind generator to power it all. A feature in the *San Francisco Chronicle* opened a door to the Design Loft at Stanford University and the know-how to replace the defective gearbox and exposed propeller shaft with a new and improved propulsion system. As part of their fall semester project, the engineering students devised a stainless steel box positioned in front of the pedaller, through which an all-in-one pedal unit could be lowered and secured below the waterline. The unit itself was shaped like an outboard motor, only smaller and with pedals in place of an engine. Instead of being pushed from astern, *Moksha* would now be pulled amidships by a forward-mounted "tractor" propeller. Gone was the need for a skeg, deep-sea seal, and marine bearing, all paraphernalia at risk of being damaged or going wrong. Friction losses were reduced, and an emergency spare could be dropped into service at a moment's notice—no more white-knuckle episodes being blown onto coral reefs! Completing

---

* Although somewhat draconian, the treatment worked. The vascular sheath of connective tissue known as the periosteum had been stripped from my left tibia on impact with Wilbur Ladd's Cadillac. Using needles to conduct electricity deep into the leg was a simple but effective way to stimulate the periosteum to grow back by resuming the supply of blood and other healing properties to the bone fragments. Months later, I was given the all clear on both legs, avoiding the dreaded bone graft operation.

the upgrade were two beautiful propellers, custom designed by the Oceanographic Department at MIT and lovingly handcrafted out of stainless steel by a local craftsman, Scott Morrison.*

Joined by an assortment of friends and acquaintances, setting in motion our new policy of inclusiveness, we tried out the new system on a hundred-mile jaunt down the coast to Monterey. Commodore Pitney accompanied me on the first leg, following a predictably boozy send-off from the Bay View Boat Club. What should have been a two-hour cakewalk to the north side of the Golden Gate, carried out of the Bay on the afternoon tide, ended up going wildly awry. Our newly acquired GPS never made it on board, so when the fog rolled in, we became hopelessly lost. Not that a GPS would've made much difference, as it turned out. On his third loop of Alcatraz Island, Arf announced that he'd forgotten to bring his glasses and was unable to see the compass.

It was nearly midnight by the time we rolled into the marina at Fort Baker, met by Arf's near-hysterical partner, Barbara, sobbing on the dockside.

Stuart, recently arrived from Florida to help with fundraising, co-pedalled the penultimate section from Santa Cruz to Moss Landing. Then it was the turn of professional photographer Theresa Ortolani, a Portuguese-Italian beauty with raven hair, olive skin, and a smile that could bring down empires. We'd met at *Moksha's* inaugural launch, posing in the cockpit for a photo. Bare arms touched. Sparks flew. By November, we were living together.

It was a blissful day pedalling across Monterey Bay. So blissful in fact that we did it naked, covering up before the *Monterey Herald* cameraman picked us out from the end of the pier with his telephoto lens.

---

* We'd used a powerboat to pull *Moksha* around Pueblo Reservoir, towing her on the end of a fish scale. Measuring her hull resistance at various speeds allowed the technicians at MIT to calculate the optimum propeller size, shape, and pitch. The result was two-bladed and fourteen inches in diameter.

Moksha was hauled out and trailered to her temporary new home of the Monterey Maritime Museum, where an open-air exhibit provided Stuart with a fundraising platform until she was needed in Peru. The new propulsion system had meanwhile performed flawlessly, upping *Moksha's* speed by more than twenty per cent, a figure that would mean seventy fewer pedalling days on the Pacific. As our late mentor Peter Bird once advised: "The less time spent on the water, the better your chances of survival."

The only thing missing was Steve. Earlier in December, he and Eilbhe had travelled to Dublin to visit her family and to take a break from the expedition. The strain of holding on all those months, living hand to mouth while waiting for me to catch up from Colorado, had taken its toll. He was on the verge of burnout.

"It was all meant to be some kind of liberation," he reminded me before leaving. "From mediocrity and the trappings of shallow, consumer society. That's why we called the boat *Moksha*, right?"

I nodded, feeling a stab of guilt.

"But now I feel more enslaved than ever, to debt and the insatiable appetite of this monster we've created. I'm not ready to quit. I just need to prove to myself that I can walk away from it, that I still have a choice between wanting to do it, and having to do it."

Central America
Love in the Baja

Plans are deliberately indefinite, more to travel than to arrive anywhere.
—Robert Pirsig, *Zen and the Art of Motorcycle Maintenance*

"THAT'S THE LAST ONE," whispered Jenny as the patrol car rumbled past. We watched the red taillights disappear north towards Big Sur, and the dark closed in again. "Time to wake the Frenchies," I said.

Olly and Carole were sleeping soundly in the bushes behind us, blissfully unaware of the vigil that Jenny and I had kept since sunset. It was now two in the morning. We had four hours to ride the twenty-five miles to Gorda before the cops came back.

At any other time of year this would have been a doddle on Highway 1, but a succession of winter storms had blocked the coast road with landslides in half a dozen places. The way south was closed to all traffic, according to the boot-faced policeman we'd spoken to earlier.

"Anyone trying to sneak past will automatically go to jail," he'd warned, eyeing our bikes suspiciously. Our only option, apparently, was to backtrack to Monterey and take a 300-mile detour via Highway 101. This posed a monumental pain, not least because we'd already gone fifty miles in the wrong direction.

Bugger that for a game of soldiers, we'd all agreed.

We were four. My old friend Olly Briche had recently arrived from the south of France, where we'd last seen each other two summers before. "Zer froggies are joining zis ultimate 'uman-powered nightmare," he'd informed me in an email, "to 'elp your zorry rosbif-ass to Peru." Joining him was his irresistibly zesty girlfriend Carole, a laugh riot of wild hair and flashing teeth. Together they made for a delightful couple: very French, very easy-going. On a practical level, Carole's Spanish language skills offered a valuable opportunity to introduce our educational programmes to schools along the way.

Then there was Jenny, a twenty-three-year-old Minnesotan I'd met while presenting to the Redwood City Yacht Club. At my invitation for audience members to join the upcoming leg, she'd raised her hand and tentatively enquired about selection criteria. Jenny was overweight, new to cycling, and a self-professed homebody. She was duly welcomed as the fourth member.

I'd also hoped a fifth person would join, a sylphlike siren starting to get under my skin. But nothing was ever simple with Theresa. In spite of our blossoming romance, I'd only got a taste of the honey. The reason? Ian McLaughlin, a source of unrequited love and former heartache, the reason she'd run away from New York in the first place.

Rousing Olly and Carole, we packed up our gear and began freewheeling down the road towards Gorda. Sounds became amplified in the darkness: waves crashing on the rocks below, water splashing up from our tyres, and our hearts hammering with the rush that comes from intentionally breaking the law.

A ROAD CLOSED sign loomed. We dismounted and wheeled our bikes to where the tarmac ended abruptly. A short ravine led to a sunken mud and boulder field where the road used to be. Hugging the landward side where the drop-off was less severe, we steered our heavily laden bikes down into the mire.

Then, sod's law, the heavens opened. Silent panic set in as we slipped and cursed our way across terrain capable of giving way at any second, sweeping us into the Pacific. I glanced back at Jenny. Her spanking new bike and spotless panniers were now coated in wet clay, and her face, deathly white in the moonlight, betrayed a cornucopia of competing emotions—uncertainty, fear, and exhilaration.

"This is more like it." She giggled nervously.

Four and a half hours later, tired, filthy, and soaked to the skin, we pushed our rigs up and over one last mudslide and entered the tiny hamlet of Gorda. Dawn was breaking as we passed a road crew starting for the day. A barrel-chested gorilla in an orange hard hat looked us up and down like we'd just crawled out of a hole in the ground—which, in a way, we had.

"And where in the hell do you guys think you're going?" he challenged, knowing full well we'd come from Monterey illegally.

"Lima, Peru!" cried Jenny, grinning exuberantly.
And we all had a good laugh at that.

CLINGING TO THE edge of the North American continent, as if by un-
earthly will in some places, Highway 1 weaves its way down the Big Sur
coast for more than a hundred rugged, windswept miles before levelling out to the lowland valleys around San Luis Obispo. This section
was always going to be arduous kitted out with full panniers (the road
seldom stayed horizontal for more than a dozen paces before snaking
up and around another jagged headland), but pedalling a 1968 Raleigh
3-speed, my mount of choice to South America, promised a whole new
take on the meaning of suffering. Also to come were the searing deserts
of Mexico, the stifling rainforests of Chiapas, El Salvador, Costa Rica,
and Nicaragua, and the grinding switchbacks of the Pan American
Highway through Ecuador and Peru.

My decision to use such an antediluvian contraption rested in the
same logic behind donning rollerblades to cross the United States. Different modes of propulsion alter the experience of travel, shaping perception of people and places, and I found that the slower the pace, the
richer the encounters. A three-speed clunker was, admittedly, taking
this theory to the extreme, however I detested expedited locomotion for
the sake of it. The idea of staring at asphalt for months on end just to
set a speed record left me cold.

On January 29, another storm blew in from the south. We spent a
long, tiresome day ploughing into the driving rain and buffeting headwind. Carole had it especially hard, handicapped as she was with a junk
bicycle found rusting in the back of someone's garage in Santa Cruz.
As the afternoon wore on, she complained increasingly of chaffing and
started falling farther behind.

Dusk came early, robbing us of sight like a gathering glaucoma. We stopped to consider our options. Either we set up tents in the pouring rain, or push on to the town of San Simeon. The former was the sensible option, of course. Everyone was beat. But the decision was ultimately made for us. Out of the swirling mist a sign took shape: SAN SIMEON - 6 MILES.

"Hey, ma man!" Olly called to me. "We are nearly zere."

Hopes and spirits revitalized, we affixed headlamps and red blinker lights and pressed on. Half an hour passed. And another. After an hour and a half, San Simeon was still nowhere in sight.

Rolling to a stop in the middle of the road, Jenny checked her bike computer. "Jeez, we've done thirteen miles since that last sign."

"I think I know what's happened," I said grimly. "Someone must've tampered with it. I bet there used to be a 1 in front of the 6."

Olly's face fell. "You mean, it woz double figure? What kind of azzhole would do sumsing like zat?"

"Obviously one with a *hilarious* sense of humour," Jenny muttered in disgust.

The rain was still coming down like stair rods, and the night clung to us like a damp veil. Only our pale complexions reflected in the beams of the flashlights cut the ragged darkness.

Carole suddenly cottoned on to what had happened. "So you sink … eez really six*teen* miles to San Simeon?"

"Or if it was a 2 in front of the 6 it could be twenty six," I replied.

This was the final straw for poor Carole. "Ooof! Zis ees really too much." She threw up her arms in defeat. "I 'ave fucked up 'ands. I 'ave fucked up kneez. H'and now"—she made a face and shifted awkwardly—"I 'ave fucked up puzzy." The rest of us just stood there, speechless at the revelation. "Most of awl," the petite Frenchwoman continued angrily, "I am tired of zis … fucked up piss off sheet!" And with that she dismounted, launched her bicycle into the hedge, and started marching off in the direction of San Simeon, grumbling loudly as she went.

"C'est vraiment de la MERDE, *cette histoire d'avancer avec sa seule énergie humaine. Olive, pourquoi m'as tu embarquée dans cette galère?"**

And so on.

Three miles later, the lights of San Simeon emerged from the fog like luminous cotton balls. We hit the liquor store as it was closing and descended on the first motel with a hot tub. Sixty dollars for a room wasn't cheap, even between four of us, but Carole was close to mutiny by this point.

We ended up paying full price for sneaking through the landslide area, too. By the time we arrived in San Luis Obispo the following afternoon, our bodies had become a mass of raised welts and weeping sores. Jenny's arms and legs were so badly blistered she had to go to hospital for steroid shots. The cause? The bushes we'd used to hide from the cops, infested with poison oak.

Pushing south, the incessant rain tapered off, and, coupled with improving fitness and the flatter, straighter roads, our daily mileages steadily increased. We took to camping on the beach, falling asleep to the surf murmuring on the shore, and waking at first light to blushing pinks and a sickle moon hanging in the west.

Oxnard Beach was one such morning. Before thinking about it too much, I crawled out of my sleeping bag and ran naked into the ice-cold water. That first wave punched the air clean out of my lungs, leaving me gasping for precious oxygen like the first breath of life.

I'm alive. Yes, really alive!

Heat flooding from my core, I strode back into camp feeling like a Viking warrior. The first order of the day was to get the stove going for tea. Then porridge, supplemented with the usual quota of teeth-crunching sand. As we rolled up our sleeping bags and prepared to hit the trail, a mob of screeching seagulls appeared overhead, dive-bombing the leftovers.

---

* This is really crap, a human-powered nightmare to be sure. Olly, why did I let you talk me into this?

"Watch zis," said Olly, lobbing one of my sandals in the air. A gull immediately swooped in and snatched it.

I watched with growing dismay as my flying footwear drifted farther and farther down the beach, seized from one greedy beak to the next. "That's my sandal, you froggie bastard," I protested. Eventually, it fell, not the juicy morsel the birds thought it was after all.

"Gives a whole new meaning to waiting for the other shoe to drop," laughed Jenny.

Camping was forbidden where we found ourselves two nights later, sitting on the Venice Beach boardwalk, sharing a bottle of Old Milwaukee. It was late, and the heaving metropolis of Los Angeles stretched another fifty miles to the south. We would have to keep riding through the night to find somewhere to sleep.

Olly nodded to the row of mansions behind us. "I wonder 'ow much one of zees cost."

It was prime beachfront real estate, each property worth several million dollars. The nearest one had a FOR SALE sign posted. The curtains were drawn and the place looked deserted.

Hopping over the white picket fence, I crept around to the side door, which, incredibly, had been left unlocked. No alarm system, either. Five minutes later, we had all the bikes parked in the kitchen and our sleeping bags rolled out on the living room floor. A splinter of yellow light filtered in from the streetlamp outside. Otherwise, it was completely dark. No one dared use a flashlight.

"Only Hollywood A-list accommodation for us," sniggered Jenny.

But good things never last, of course. Our brush with affluence came to an abrupt halt at 8:00 am the next morning. The front door swung open, and a suit carrying a clipboard breezed in, prospective buyer in tow. The real estate agent did a double take at the scene before him.

Jenny and I were enjoying a lie-in, lounging in our sleeping bags, while Carole brewed up coffee in the kitchen. Olly, meanwhile, was having a BM in the adjoining bathroom, whistling contentedly with the door ajar. It was a freeze-frame of our typical morning routine. Only on this occasion we happened to be inside a house.

The agent's eyes narrowed. "You have two minutes before I call the cops," he hissed.

Ensenada, Mexico, April 7

AFTER CLEARING CUSTOMS and immigration in Tijuana, we hightailed it south, aiming to put as many miles as possible between ourselves and a border region renowned for thievery, narcotics, and gun-wielding banditry in general. We rolled into Ensenada that evening, bought fresh fish from the night market, *el mercado de mariscos,* and had it barbecued at a nearby food stand. Four fish tacos with guacamole and cabbage for four pesos, just fifty cents per person. *Cervezas* followed. We'd made it to Mexico, after all! And despite my earlier request to have sex with two large fishermen *(Me gusta dos pescadores grande)* instead of ordering two large fish tacos *(Me gusta dos tacos grandes de pescado),* we'd negotiated our first Mexican meal, Carole's Spanish saving the day.

Wobbling happily out of town, our bellies full and feeling slightly tipsy, we looked for somewhere to camp. A narrow track appeared, darkened field looming beyond. We took it. Too tired to set up tents, we simply piled the bikes together, rolled out our sleeping bags, and fell asleep. In the morning, five panniers were missing.

"I don't believe it," Carole wailed. "Zer bastards. Zey took my camera and awl my feelm."

"My front panniers, too," said Jenny, picking through what was left. "My medical pack is gone. Tools. Stove. Spare cycling shorts. Mug. Oh crap, and my journal!"

None of my bags had been taken, amazing considering how

accessible they were (my bike was at the top of the pile). The thieves had missed out on a laptop, two camcorders, and a still camera.

"It doesn't make sense," I mentioned to a security guard later that morning. We were standing outside a supermarket, watching the bikes while my teammates shopped for replacement gear. "They stole something from everyone else's bicycle. Why not mine?"

The guard, an older man with grey hamster moustache, wagged a knowing finger at me. "Because they are pious men, *Señor.*"

"Thieves, pious? I don't think so."

He pointed to the plastic figurine I kept as a mascot secured with duct tape to the Raleigh's handlebars. It had come free with a meal from a Taco Bell in San Diego, part of a promotional campaign for the newly released Star Wars movie. *"Mira, Señora de Guadalupe."*

Dressed all in white, hair done up in her signature buns, Princess Leia did, admittedly, emanate an air of saintliness.

"She is holding the cross of her son, *Jesús.*"

I peered closer. Cradled in the tomboy's arms was a lightsaber—albeit a bad rendition of one. Being a cheap toy, the space-age weapon had obviously been mistaken for a crucifix by the thieves.

The guard lowered his voice deferentially. "Even *ladrones* would never steal from the Blessed Virgin Mary."

Our route took us 500 miles down the Baja Peninsula, the slender digit of land suspended below California and separated from mainland Mexico by the Sea of Cortez. Dull, flat farmland soon gave way to scintillating desert. South of Rosario, we slogged to the top of the central plateau and entered the Catavina Boulder Field. Giant cannonballs of granite littered the surrounds, interspersed by myriad species of spiny cacti posturing at the sky like the feisty multi-armed goddess of destruction, Kali.

Which was fitting, as ninety miles north of Bahia de los Angeles, a Chevy Blazer with US licence plates pulled over and out stepped another goddess with no less thorny issues.

By this point in the journey, I'd put Theresa almost completely out of my mind. She and Ian had reunited, settled down, bought a house, got kids on the way—blah, blah, blah. They were getting on with the business of living happily ever after. End of story, Jackanory.

In reality, funding had come through from a tech company, Tandem Computers, to launch a photographic project styled after the Video Exchange Program. Kids along the route would use point-and-shoot cameras to record their world, with the results displayed in exhibitions and arranged into photo albums to be exchanged with their peers in other countries. A successful pilot with the Richmond Arts Center had landed sponsorship secured through our newly formed 501(c)(3) non-profit organization.

Ian was behind the wheel, and for one heart-stopping moment I thought he was also joining the expedition—the thought of those two going at it in the next tent over was more than I could stomach. But it soon became clear they were going their own separate ways. The group camped in the dunes that night, and in the morning, Ian began the long journey back to San Francisco and then home to New York.

They can't be that reunited, I thought, a glimmer of hope reigniting.

THE SEA OF Cortez is one of the most schizophrenic bodies of water in the world. One minute it's as smooth as silk, the next a screaming shit fight. The currents between islands run at eight knots during spring tides. El Norte winds come barrelling down the gulf without warning, whipping the sea into a maelstrom. And if you find yourself in trouble, you're as good as sunk. The closest thing to a coastguard is in Honolulu, 2,400 miles away.

In spite of this (or, perhaps, because of it—we were all rather bored of biking and craved some excitement), we planned to kayak 140 miles down the east coast from Bahia de los Angeles to a narrowing of the gulf at San Francisquito, then use the Midriff Islands to hop the sixty miles to Bahia Kino on the mainland side. In all it would take a couple of weeks, we reckoned. Three tops.

Of course there were a few minor details to straighten out before we could get underway. We didn't have any kayaks. None of us knew how to use one properly even if we did. And a hefty question mark hung over the means by which our bikes would make it to the other side. But what we lacked in forethought, we made up for in blind presumptuousness. Plus we had a secret weapon, one guaranteed to get things done in a predominantly male fishing community like Bahia de los Angeles.

Women.

Carole, Jenny, and Theresa quickly mustered an enthusiastic taskforce of male admirers. An American white water canoe instructor holidaying with his father taught us safety drills in the shallows next to their beach camp. John Weed was in his early forties, bearded, with a sinewy frame and pronounced limp. Up for an adventure, he offered to be our guide and loan me his spare kayak to complement the three sit-on-tops we'd managed to hire locally. It was through John—who, in all fairness, recognized a catastrophe waiting to happen—that we met Ed Gillette, another veteran kayaker who'd paddled from California to Hawaii in sixty days. Pulling up on the beach one evening with a commercial kayak party in tow, Ed offered his bible for the region, a nautical almanac armed with enough information to keep us from drowning any sooner than we had to: tide tables, charts, current strengths and directions, seasonal wind patterns, and so forth.

The final piece of the puzzle was meeting Gil and Mario Romero, a father-son duo who volunteered to deliver our bikes and the balance of the provisions to San Francisquito in their fishing boat. A day spent re-tarring the roof of their bungalow seemed a more than reasonable trade.

Five days after rolling up with nothing but chapped arses and a woolly idea, we hit the water, paddling in formation across the mirrored Bay of Angels towards Horse Head Island five miles to the east. Olly and Carole manned a blue sit-on-top double, their sleeping bags and dry clothes wrapped in plastic rubbish sacks and secured with bungee cords. Theresa and Jenny paddled a purple and yellow single respectively—Jenny looking as alarmed at the transition to waterborne travel as she had leaving Monterey on a bicycle all those weeks ago. The only one of us who looked right at home was John, a centaur-like hybrid of half-man, half-boat scything effortlessly along in his rudderless white water canoe.

Behind us, the desiccated Baja hills rose above a muddle of whitewashed buildings marking the town. I stopped to snap a photo, and then sat watching the others pull away like moths to the rising sun, their silhouetted paddle blades rising and falling against the glare. Noticing Theresa's outline off to the right, I felt a pang. For our entire time in Bahia, she'd kept her distance.

Looks like we're back to being just friends, I thought ruefully.

Up close there was nothing remotely equine about Isla Cabeza de Caballo, just an array of decapitated sharks' heads grinning ghoullike from the beach, the unwanted remains tossed by fishermen. Random carcasses rotted in the shallows. Death festooned the rocky shore. And when I scrambled to higher ground to scope out our route down the coast, I came face to face with the recently severed head of a gull perched in a hollow in the cliff, its lifeless eyes staring stiffly out to sea.

Unnerved, but determined not to lose the euphoria of setting out, the group climbed back in the boats and immediately engaged in a furious water fight, flinging great paddlefuls and hooting with glee. I caught a crab and was upside down in a flash, floundering in the freezing water. The drill John had taught us for assisted recovery—banging on the underside of the hull—kicked in immediately, but no one could manoeuvre in time. Lungs close to bursting, I had to tear the Velcro seal from my cockpit and bail out.

After three hours of paddling, I was still shivering. The day, which had started out bright, was now overcast, the sun lurking behind an impenetrable curtain of cloud. The translucent water turned the colour of red wine, and a brisk breeze pawed at my shirt, sucking the remaining heat from my body.

"You okay?" said Theresa, rafting up alongside. "Oh my goodness, you're white as a sheet!"

"Freezing," I hissed.

The rest of the party was already out of sight around the next headland, El Pescador, aiming to make camp before nightfall.

Theresa reached for my wrist with her spare hand. "Your heart rate's a bit slow," she said anxiously. "It's probably hypothermia kicking in from that capsize. You better get to shore, Jase. Take off those wet clothes."*

The sandy beaches around Bahia had petered out the farther south we'd paddled, morphing into an uninviting jumble of fist-sized rocks banking sharply into the sea. Landing awkwardly, I hauled my yellow kayak up to the high tide mark, stripped off my clothes, and clawed naked into my sleeping bag.

A minute later, I heard the clatter of rocks and turned to see Theresa pull her boat up beside mine and teeter barefoot over to where I was lying. Even with a frumpy kayak skirt bouncing around her waist like a thrift store ballerina, she looked lovely.

"Doing any better, Jase?"

My teeth were still chattering. Steve was right: I was worse than useless in the cold. *Never mind the Bering Straits*, I thought bitterly. *I can't even cross the Sea of fucking Cortez in springtime without freezing to death.*

---

* Hypothermia, the number one killer in and around the water: core temperature plummets, extremities turn blue, the skin becomes blotchy, the pulse weak and irregular. Below 77°F, the pupils become fixed and reflexes cease. Cardiac arrest and death soon follow.

"Can't … seem to … get warm," I mumbled, blowing vigorously into the folds of my hood.

The zipper slid open. Cold air poured inside the bag.

"What the—?"

Theresa's body felt warm and supple. She was naked, her skin smelling lightly of salt and lavender soap. I wrapped my arms around her waist, buried my face into the small of her neck, and spooned my body into hers.

God bless hypothermia, I thought, and smiled.

So BEGAN TEN days of unbridled indulgence in the four lubricious *esses:* sun, sea, sand, and sex, a heady cocktail if administered in the right order.

By day we paddled the emerald sea, escorted by pods of spinning dolphins and anxious seals punching their whiskery snouts beside the boats, snorting and huffing like startled horses. Shoals of steel-bellied mackerel, hunted from the deep, churned the middle distance into a rolling cauldron. Gannets wowed us with heart-stopping plunges, wings folding back at the last second. And once, as Theresa and I paddled together, laughing, joking, and belting out bad opera with snatches of Johnny Cash's *A Boy Name Sue,* we heard the unmistakable sound of whales blowing in the milky haze. Paddling hard for twenty minutes, we intercepted a family of finbacks heading south from the calving lagoons. They surfaced on collision course, one behind the other, and for one tense moment it looked as if they might ram us. The lead animal took one final gasp a mere stone's throw away, and then dove, the others disappearing in its wake, leaving a stale fetor hanging in an otherwise breathless afternoon.

Occasionally, the coastline turned up unexpected treasures, like the secret cave that Olly discovered one morning. A labyrinthine tunnel led to a natural cathedral hewn from the living rock. Drifting silently across the subterranean lagoon, our heads cocked back, we marvelled at the granite arches spanning overhead. A shimmering crypt opened up beneath us, pulsating with kaleidoscopic throngs of swaying sponges, sea anemones, and flitting fish. Regiments of crimson and purple crabs marched up and down the pillars of dripping rock like the playing card soldiers in Alice in Wonderland. It was Jacques Cousteau meets William S. Burroughs in the psychedelic school bus of *The Electric Kool-Aid Acid Test.*

Towards the end of each day, as we neared our target of seventeen miles, John, an accomplished angler as well as expert paddler, trailed a fishing line. Bass and snapper would be flapping three ranks deep by the time the rest of us pulled up on the beach. Then, the evening routine would begin: wood gathered, fire lit, rice or couscous prepared, and the fish barbecued in hot coals.

Some nights we'd sit quietly after a meal, gazing into the fire or up to the heavens, passing around a bottle of Cuervo Gold and musing at our extraordinary good fortune to be where we were in the universe at that particular moment, doing what we were doing. Other nights would be drowned in discordant percussion, everyone beating the hell out of a saucepan lid, frying pan, or empty water container. The cacophony drove waves of scorpions and wolf spiders out of the driftwood in protest, scuttling over sandy toes and sending the Frenchies screeching for cover like a pair of scalded cats.

The good times weren't to last, however. Approaching the fish camp at San Rafael, friction began mounting over the frequency of layover days. John, at first distracted by the bouncing tits and unabashed nudity, had become exasperated by the holiday pace.

We woke on the morning of the eleventh day to the sound of a motorboat shadowing the shore. It was Gil and Mario, looking for us in *Acapulco.* The ponga was laden with our bicycles, food, and fresh water stored in fifty-five-gallon drums. Jenny paddled out to meet them while the rest of us dithered on the beach, arguing how best to get everything unloaded. The wind, meanwhile, started to freshen.

Ten minutes went by. "Hey, guys!" shouted Gil. "We're gonna head over to the cove at San Francisquito. Find shelter before this wind comes to anything."

But it was already too late. Like the hand of God, El Norte came whistling out of the north, whipping the sea into eight-foot standing waves. Gil gunned the throttle and threw the tiller hard over. I had my back turned when it happened. Olly whispered, *"Oh merde,"* and I looked back in time to see *Acapulco* corkscrewing off the crest of a wave at fifteen knots and landing belly-up in a curtain of white foam.

Then all hell broke loose.

John had his boat in the water first, paddle glinting as he tore to reach the bodies in the water. Olly and I snatched lifejackets before launching the double like a two-man bobsleigh. Carole ran up and down the beach without a stitch on, flapping her arms and yelling, *"Oh sheet! Oh sheet! Oh sheet!"*

Theresa was off in the dunes somewhere, taking photos.

It was a miracle no one drowned. Jenny, who'd been hitching a ride on *Acapulco* at the time, was the first to reach safety, towed to shore on the back of John's red single. By the time Olly and I arrived, Gil and Mario had managed to crawl onto the upturned keel of their stricken craft and were hanging on for dear life, white bum-cheeks exposed, sombreros flailing in the wind.

In the end, the only casualty was *Acapulco*. As the day wore on, and our efforts to flip her right side up grew increasingly desperate, she drifted closer and closer to the reef system downwind. By evening, all we could do was stand helplessly and watch the awful business of a boat, that hybrid personality of wood, resins, hopes, and dreams, grind itself to smithereens on the rocks.

Gil was remarkably philosophical about the whole fiasco. No one had been killed, he pointed out, and the rest was just stuff—replaceable. "Besides," he added almost cheerily, "I've crashed a few boats into this coastline over the years. You might have seen some of them on your way down here."

We had. A long line of them, sixteen in total, marooned on the beach like sun-bleached whale skeletons.

Gil's shipwrecking history aside, I knew the blame for *Acapulco's* demise ultimately rested on my own shoulders. Democracy is a nice idea if you have time for it, but when the shit hits the fan, preservation of life and equipment depends on the right of veto by one person. It was a lesson that should have sunk in on the Atlantic. Now I would never forget it.

For the next three days, El Norte kept us pinned down in the dunes, unable to take to the boats. A makeshift shelter bodged together with paddles and a salvaged tarpaulin shielded us from the wind, sun, and flying sand. One of the fifty-five-gallon drums filled with fresh water rolled ashore, along with several packets of gasoline-soaked biscuits. Then, on the second afternoon, a young fisherman wandered into camp carrying a net bag filled with octopus, lobster, and squid. Gustavo was shy with curly black hair and a torn polo neck. He spoke not a word of English. The next evening he came again, walking the six-mile round trip from the fish camp, this time bearing yellowtail snapper. He refused to accept any payment for his offerings. After de-scaling the fish, he squatted by the fire, stroking his coal-black moustache and chatting to Carole in Spanish.

"He sez 'e eez honouring an awld tradition," Carole translated. "To 'elp zose in trouble wiz zer sea."

That night, coyotes circled nearby, barking and yipping. John woke in the early hours to see a dark form standing over Mario's sleeping form. Their tracks were everywhere in the morning. A five-gallon container filled with precious drinking water lay punctured on the beach, and a pilfered PowerBar chewed and spat out in disgust. Examining her kayak, Carole found a bag of her expensive French lingerie missing, leading us on a tantalizing trail of bedroom paraphernalia strewn down the beach. Baja coyotes were evidently picky when it came to energy bars and underwear.

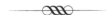

SOMETHING SHIFTED IN the group dynamic after that. Nobody said anything, but the sinking of *Acapulco* signalled Party Over. No more lounging around in the sun baking tits 'n bums. Olly and Carole announced the novelty of living out of a kayak to be wearing thin, in any case. Upon our arrival in San Francisquito, they took their bikes and rode south to La Paz. They'd take the ferry to Mazatlan, they said, and meet up with us on the road to Guadalajara. Jenny, too, craved a change. She was ready to fly the nest and strike out on her own adventure without any set agenda.

"Travelling in a group, you're always having to compromise," she noted sombrely. "I didn't realize how difficult that would be."

I clicked her picture before she, Gil, and Mario hitched a ride back to Bahia in the local ice truck. Her expedition tee shirt, the same pristine one she'd acquired at the end of my Redwood City talk, was now unrecognizably filthy. Her bike was also trashed: dented, scuffed, and caked in dust. I cast my mind back to the woman setting out from Monterey all those months ago, her gear immaculate, legs white and flabby. The greenhorn had seemed so far out of her comfort zone, I'd secretly wondered how far she would actually get. The "after" photo, sitting with Theresa under a thatched *palapa*, portrayed a very different person. Jenny was now tanned and thirty pounds lighter, her sassy smile oozing with confidence.

That left John, Theresa, and me to tackle the sixty miles to Bahia Kino on the mainland side. Gustavo appeared at the last minute, begging to come along. He was tired of life at the fish camp, according to his bilingual friend, Berto, and yearned to travel. After all that the fisherman had done for us, how could we refuse?

The first hop was thirteen miles to the island of San Lorenzo. Having consulted the tide tables in Ed Gillette's almanac, we slipped out of San Francisquito cove at midnight—Theresa and Gustavo paddling the double, John and me singles—aiming to cross the fast-flowing channel at low tide. Navigating at night without compass or GPS meant relying on moonlight to monitor the shadowy nub of land ahead and the promontory of Punta San Gabriel behind. It was dark still when we made landfall on the rocky shore and slumped groggy with fatigue on our air mattresses. The next slack water was in six hours, two full turns of the tide since leaving San Francisquito.

By dusk the following evening, we were skirting the northern tip of Isla Esteban, the midmost island, looking for a spot to camp. A section of beach with space above the high tide mark materialized in the gloom, but something didn't seem right. Was the beach moving? As we paddled closer, the grey shoreline twitched and wriggled like a corpse teeming with maggots. Indistinct shapes morphed into granite boulders, rocking and swaying in the twilight. Then the picture became clear.

The entire beach was covered in an orgy of gasping, barging sea lions. The smell was incredible.

John and I stopped paddling and watched. The larger ones, presumably alpha males, made powerful lunges at each other, snarling and biting, setting their flanks wobbling with the exertion. The prospect of sleeping anywhere near the clumsy brutes struck me as perilous in the extreme. What else to do, though? It would be dark in less than fifteen minutes. The only other option was to keep going, with no guarantee of finding another campsite.

I turned to John. "We'll just have to get them to budge up a bit, eh?"

"Actually, they're a protected species, Jason, and this is their natural habitat." This nugget of information was delivered in the dismissive tone of an admonishing schoolmaster. "We should definitely keep going."

John had appointed himself Safety Officer from the start, which was fine, since the rest of us were clueless. But sometimes his fussing went too far. We'd just paddled thirty miles in eighteen hours and Gustavo, his first time in a kayak, looked utterly spent. We were all tired, hungry, and losing body heat.

Irritation flared in my throat. "We *need* to get out of these boats, John."

"But it's against the law."

"Fuck the law. This is Mexico!"

"That doesn't mean we can do whatever the hell we want."

At any other time, I would have willingly conceded that John had a point. The way gringos waltzed over the border, behaving as they pleased, gave outsiders a bad name. On this occasion, however, his lecturing infuriated me. Ever since leaving Bahia de los Angeles, he and I had clashed over key decisions. His matter-of-fact, *I-know-better-than-you* take on sea lions was the final straw.

"This is fucking bullshit, John."

"Calm down, Jason. You're beginning to sound—"

"Sound like what?"

"Like an eco-terrorist."

An eco-terrorist? I could only mouth the words for choking fury.

"Hey, hey, what's going on?" said Theresa, pulling alongside with Gustavo.

Sensing I was about to explode with Krakatoan consequences, I kept my mouth shut while John explained the dilemma. "Jason thinks we should clear the sea lions off the beach so we can rest. I say we keep going. Maybe there's another beach around the corner? This is their habitat. We shouldn't disturb them."

Theresa rolled her eyes. She, too, was weary from the long paddle, and there was little love lost between John and her, anyway.

"Listen, John," she said icily. "They're sea lions. They live in water. They'll just go somewhere else."

Judging by his pained expression, the kayak instructor clearly regretted ever agreeing to join us in the first place. He looked aggrievedly at Theresa, then at me. "Geez, what is it with you two? Everything always ends up being a pissing contest. Especially with you, Theresa. It's like you gotta argue with everything I tell you."

This was a mistake, and he knew it. The fiery diva tightened her jaw and let rip: "Well, we're not expert kayakers like you, John. And I don't know about anybody else, but right now I'm fuckin' exhausted."

A furious commotion interrupted us, a great barking and splashing and clattering of rocks. Gustavo, who'd been quietly waiting for *los gringos locos* to quit squabbling and make camp, had finally lost patience, slipped into the water, and was now marching up the beach, shooing the sea lions into the surf.

The situation defused itself immediately. As a local fisherman and frequent visitor to these islands, Gustavo had no doubt coexisted with sea lions for much of his life. The harsh reality of eking out a living from the sea didn't allow for long, drawn-out discussions to reach consensus. Nor did it lend itself to showering universal love and kindness on every reeking sea lion in the North Pacific. And what could the rest of us say to that?

THE FOLLOWING AFTERNOON, perhaps in divine retribution for international crimes against sea lions, the camp stove exploded in my face.

A cracked O-ring in the fuel canister was the outward cause. Having pumped the plunger to build pressure, I was lighting the fuel in the primer cup when a stream of petrol spurted out and drenched the right side of my face. A split second later, my head was on fire.

All I remember was hitting the beach and burying my face in the sand to suffocate the flames. Except there was no sand, only rocks, and the petrol kept burning, blistering my flesh to the consistency of bubble wrap.

With second-degree burns and only a basic medical kit between us, it was critical to reach Kino before infection set in. El Norte, not surprisingly, had other ideas. As we paddled into Dog Bay on the south side of Isla Tiburon, the last of the stepping stone islands, the miscreant northerly struck with all its by-now familiar, ugly fury.

A fishing shack cobbled together from driftwood offered protection of sorts (we'd left our tents in San Francisquito to save weight and make better time). The roof rattled, the walls creaked, and the mood of the group began to founder as the day wore on. John and I were barely speaking as it was, and Gustavo's pinched expression suggested that life in the fish camp was looking better by the minute. Even Theresa and I were on the skids, Theresa frustrated at having to paddle the double with Gustavo instead of with me. To cap it all, we were almost out of drinking water. We'd cut the contingency too fine.

Next morning, the wind continued to howl and foam streaked off the white caps in the bay. John and Gustavo scoured the surrounding hills for barrel cacti rich in water, but the specimens of *Ferocactus covillei* they found were too small to yield any real sustenance. That night, while the others slept, I experimented with distillation: boiling saltwater in our cooking pot hooked up to a Camelbak bladder and running the tubing through cold seawater to condense the steam. After two hours of toiling over an open fire—fingers scorched, serum from my burns dripping into the flames—I had a single cup of salt-free water.

I roused Theresa to share the good news. "Look!" I whispered, setting the mug beside her sleeping face. "It's not much, but at least we won't die of thirst."

"Yrrrrrphhmm. Wha—what was that, Jase?"

Yawning, she stretched her arms over her head and knocked the cup clean over. In the time it took for the life-saving elixir to disappear into the sand, she was back sound asleep.

The third day broke without change. We lay in the hut keeping perfectly still, breathing through our nostrils to reduce evaporation loss. Thirst is a raging tyrant once it takes hold, an all-consuming demon that devours all reason, expunging the mind of any other thought or concern. A half-empty litre of Coke stood in the corner, abandoned by a previous occupant. It was undoubtedly stale and tepid, but the bottle grew to obscene proportions in my mind. I began seeing it everywhere: on the underside of the roof, on the backs of my eyelids while I dozed. And when I awoke from quaffing icy cold sodas in my dreams, the first thing I saw was the real thing itself, all-powerful, all-pervading, as omnipotent as life itself.

No one dared touch it, though. No one wanted to be the first to crack.

By mid-afternoon, El Norte showed signs of abating. Our weather window, at last! Except that paddling the twenty-two miles to Kino in our weakened state and with no water was out of the question. Twice we heard the far-off sound of an outboard motor. Twice we stumbled out of the hut and ran to the nearest headland, waving and hollering. Both times our efforts were to no avail, the cigar-shaped pongas maintaining their unswerving trajectory across the silvery sea.

"Bastards!" cursed Theresa. "That last one was close enough to see us for sure."

"Thing is, they run drugs this way from South America," John said gloomily. "Weapons, too. There's nothing we've got that they need. For all they know we could be trying to lure them into a trap."

Accepting defeat, John, Gustavo, and I tramped back to the shack, resigned to spending the next several days distilling enough seawater to make the crossing. Theresa wandered off on her own, claiming she needed time to think.

A little later, there was a high-pitched drone of another motor. Only this time the craft seemed to be drawing nearer, not further away. I poked my head out of the hut. A ponga was, indeed, heading towards us, but it wasn't until I reached the top of the headland that I saw why. Theresa was jumping up and down on the beach, waving something in the air.

Her skirt.

WE WERE SITTING in the shade of a red bougainvillea in Chi Chi and Marilyn's garden when word came through on their high-frequency radio set. Javier's ponga was on its way from San Francisquito to deliver our bikes and pick up the kayaks. It would be with us later that afternoon.

Time was running out. One way or the other, Theresa had to make up her mind. Either she returned to her former life with Ian, or rode south with me.

Three days before, having persuaded a bewildered ponga crew that we actually needed water not help rescuing a half-naked *gringa,* we'd completed the crossing to Bahia Kino in a little over fourteen hours. Two American ex-pats, Chi Chi and Marilyn Rodriguez, were there to greet us on the beach. They already knew who we were.

"We were gettin' worried," said Chi Chi, scratching a bronzed belly. *"Beach Bum* said they sighted you four days ago near Esteban."

Marilyn and her husband were members of Rescue One, a neighbourhood maritime emergency service for non-Mexicans. Discrimination aside, it was reassuring to know that we'd been sighted. We stored our kayaks in their backyard and did little more than sleep and eat for the next 48 hours. A tub of silver sulfadiazine antibiotic cream sourced from a local pharmacy soothed my burns and expedited the healing process.

I took Theresa's hands in mine. "You have to be the one to decide, T. If you're not sure, maybe its best—"

"Best for what?" she snapped. "For me to go, is that what you want?'

No! A voice screamed inside me. *Of course not, I think I'm ...*

I squeezed her hands. "All I'm saying is, it should be your choice, not mine. What does your heart tell you?"

THERESA WAS WEARING the same ivory dress we'd bought in the market earlier. She looked stunning, coal-black hair ablaze against the cascade of bridal gown white. We walked barefoot, hand in hand, following the contours of the bleached shore to the rendezvous point where John and Gustavo would be waiting. Waves rushed up to greet us, fizzing excitedly around our ankles before pulling back to the sea.

"Let's make love," I whispered in her ear. She nodded, and we made for the dunes. Past gaily-coloured fishing boats bobbing in the shallows, laden with the day's catch. Past a circle of boys feverishly gutting fish, crimson streaking the sand, steel knives flashing in the remains of the day.

Suddenly, there was a shout. A boy was running up the beach, pointing behind him as he ran.

"Señor y Señora! El ponga ha llegado."

Sure enough, a torpedo shape was speeding over the horizon. A ponga, Javier's ponga, come to take away John, Gustavo, the kayaks ...

Theresa turned, her cheeks scored with tears, searching my face one last time. We'd spent a thousand lifetimes in each other's presence, saying everything there was to say without a word. When she pursed her lips, I knew.

At the water's edge, she picked up the folds of her dress, and I carried her in my arms to the waiting sea. Salt smarted my eyes, liquefying the light, dissolving everything to an incoherent blur. I kept my gaze fixed beyond the smudges of the prawn trawlers wallowing in deeper water, their outriggers beckoning in embrace. Everything slowed to a state of fugue. My head was reeling.

It's not supposed to end this way.

But my legs kept moving, matching the meter of a song drifting out across the swell from a transistor radio:

"Lonely rivers flow to the sea, to the sea.

To the open arms of the sea."

When we reached the ponga, I lifted Theresa over the gunwales and shook John and Gustavo's hands mechanically, numb to the black hole opening up inside me like a gaping maw. The skipper pulled the cord and they were gone, flying towards the dying sun. And it was only then, as her face receded into the night, the same Mexican night poised to smother me in the folds of its tenebrous cloak, and the balmy waters of the Sea of Cortez rose to my chest like a warm bath, and the chorus of that damn song kept repeating—*"And time goes by, so slowly. And time can do so much"*—adding to a loss weighing so heavily I felt my legs about to give way, that it hit me. And the realization tore through my chest like ragged claws, crushing my lungs and ripping out my heart.

For as quickly as this woman had entered my life, she was gone, and it was only now, when I knew I'd never see her again, did I realize how deeply I'd fallen in love with her, and how all I'd needed was to tell her and she would have stayed.

I RODE SOUTH to Mazatlan, six hundred long, hot, soul-destroying miles through the godforsaken desert of Sonora and Sinaloa. The folks in Bahia Kino had told me the wind always blew from the north at this time of year. That was bollocks. It was a headwind all the way, nothing save the occasional cactus to slow it down.

It hardly mattered, though. Inside I was dying. Falling apart. Dead man biking.

Why am I pedalling away from the woman I love? I thought despairingly. *Into the heart of Bumfuck Mexico on an antiquated three-speed?*

Still, the pedals kept turning, day after miserable day.

At night, I took to sleeping in flood tunnels under the road to avoid being robbed. By day, I rode on the left side of the road, against the flow of traffic. This was the suggestion of Pepe, whom we'd met in Rosarito shortly after crossing the border. Once a doctor of medicine ("Before I went crazy"), Pepe now owned a bicycle shop where we stopped to buy patches. "If a driver isn't paying attention," he explained, "you can ride off the road at the last second. From behind, you'll never know the vehicle that kills you."

It was sound advice, but that's not why I did it. There was something euphoric about the proximity of screaming cars and slamming trucks bringing me to a standstill. It fed my demons.

If only I'd told her, she would have stayed ...

I ran out of steam in the little town of Palmillas. Batteries dead, I just stood there in the afternoon heat, balls roasting on the centre frame, watching a gang of boys form a human pyramid to pick coconuts from a palm tree beside the road. When the whole lot came crashing down like a house of cards, they offered me the first gulp of their hard-won efforts. Did the town have a place to stay, I asked in halting Spanish? The youngest, Nata, took me to see his uncle, a hairdresser-cum-dance teacher who spoke good English.

"No *pensione.*" The man smiled coquettishly. "But you can stay with me if you like."

Chon, short for Ascenscion, lived in a bungalow with his brother, Angel, who was also openly gay. Whisperings of the pair taking a gringo lover spread like wildfire through the town. I didn't care. I had other plans.

Leaving the Raleigh and all my gear with the obliging brothers, I headed for the hills. I took nothing. No food. No water. No sleeping bag. Just the clothes I was standing up in. I would fast, I decided, cry for a vision like old Cheyenne Bill had described to me at the Canton Lake Pow-wow in Oklahoma, throw my dilemma out to the cosmos and see what came back.

Questions took shape as I trudged towards Cerro del Muerto, the appropriately named Mountain of Death. *Has the expedition run its course for me? Is it simply a stepping stone to the next stage of my life—to settle down with Theresa and do the things that normal people do? Or should I remain nomadic for as long as it takes to see the job through?*

After six hours of floundering up knife-edge ravines and yanking on tick-infested vegetation, I heaved myself over the topmost lip of a crag I'd spied from the valley floor. Taking off all my clothes and flicking off the hitchhikers, I sat down next to a withered cactus and began to meditate.

My plan was to sit. And sit. And sit. True vision quest means going without food or water for as long as it takes insight to come. Only I hadn't meditated in months. Since I'd arrived in San Francisco, the project's insatiable demand for time and attention—The Monster, as Steve now called the expedition—had consumed every minute of every waking day. Even out on the road there was little free time now we had a fully-grown website to feed, another mouth squalling for time. The main culprit was technology and the double-edged sword of incorporating it into the journey.

Each time my awareness wandered, I led it patiently back to the sensation of cold air passing in through my nostrils and warm air flowing out. By dark, the desperate flailing of my jellyfish-like mind was starting to subside, and the random grabbing of any brain-food morsel floating by—memories, desires, regrets, *If I could turn back the clock and tell Theresa,* etcetera—becoming less frequent. The warm glow of just being, in the moment, welled up to take its place.

But my old friend Thirst was a force yet to be reckoned with. By midnight it had become a rampaging toddler running roughshod through the mansion of my mind, bawling and shrieking. *Idiot! What were you thinking coming all the way up here without water?* My eyes bulged, and my throat burned. Like a harried parent, I stomped up and down ten flights of stairs after it, placating, sympathizing, humouring.

Night softened into day. Tired of the incessant hollering, I made a conscious effort not to be drawn anymore. I took a step back and just stared at Thirst, long enough for it to loosen its stranglehold. And from then on I had little trouble with him, or Hunger, or any other of their incorrigible cronies—Protesting Knees, Aching Back, Grumbling Stomach. I simply observed them for what they are: creations of the mind, illusions, with no innate power of their own.

On the evening of the third day, I was still sitting when the sky bruised purple and spots of rain spattered my sunburnt shoulders. A storm was brewing from the south. Donning my shorts and tee shirt, I took refuge in a crevice in the north-facing cliff until the wind backed to the northeast, forcing me to seek out new shelter. The ravine offered the only alternative. Cautiously, I lowered myself off the exposed outcrop, using the creepers to control my descent. The rain was now coming down in sheets, turning the gully to oily mire. The vine in my hands suddenly gave way. Then I was gone, freefalling into darkness.

A hundred feet of cascading mud and slashing foliage later, a nest of creepers checked my fall. I did a quick body sweep.

No serious damage. Lucky.

Still, my situation was getting desperate. Squinting into the gloom, a cavernous mouth opened up before me, a rocky overhang leading to a shallow cave. It was no Hilton, but inside it was dry and protected from the wind. I peeled off my sodden shirt to cushion my head and balled up to conserve body heat.

The storm slackened in the early hours. At first light, summoning last reserves, I re-ascended the ravine to my roost. Too weak to sit any-more, I lay on my side soaking up the sun's morning rays, watching ea-gles rise and fall on the thermals and birds of paradise swoop between the canopies far below, laughing and screeching in loud, rambunctious gangs.

It was the morning of the fourth day. I'd cried for a vision, but no vi-sion had come. No blinding revelation. No epiphany. The whole thing had been a complete and utter waste of time.

Either head back now, I told myself, *or risk becoming too weak to make it.*

Slipping into the ravine one last time, I began my descent, testing each handhold before committing weight. The gradient slowly eased, and I found myself traversing a narrow ridgeline with sheer drop-offs on either side. Painstaking care was needed not to lose footing, making it a Zen-like exercise in concentration.

Place ball down gently ... then arch ... then heel ... shift bodyweight ... pres-sure on the ball ... lift heel ... extend foot forward ...

One mistake, and I'd be in the ravine.

Ball-arch-heel ... ball-arch-heel ...

It became a mantra, every step a meditation. Before I knew it, I was walking along on a dirt path, my nostrils filled with the acrid scent of animal dung and the sweet smell of dry earth after rain.

Ball-arch-heel ... ball-arch-heel ...

Cultivated fields gave way to whitewashed buildings encircled by barricades of thorns. An old man beckoned to me from a doorway.

"Señor. Venido."

The walls of his home were bare. He was very poor. Our Lady of Guadelupe eyed me suspiciously from her corner place.

"Esperamos por usted." We were waiting for you.

I was offered plain rice and water, and signalled to rest on a string bed. Eight or more hours had passed since leaving the crag, yet I re-membered nothing of the journey.

I slept. And dreamed.

When I awoke it was dark, but in the dream all was clear. I was on the Atlantic, rocking back and forth in the cosseted confines of the Rathole, listening to the sounds of the sea. Soon it would be my turn to pedal. I didn't know how far we'd gone or how much farther we had to go. All I knew was that everything was in its place. All I needed to do was pedal.

Agonizing between the expedition and Theresa was pointless, I realized. Timing is everything in love, and that ship had sailed. The past couldn't bring back the future, and the future would only ever be an idea. Both are illusions. Only the present is real.

Ball-arch-heel ... ball-arch-heel ...

If I immersed myself in the present, decisions would continue to be made of their own accord, the right future manifesting itself like it had coming off Cerro del Muerto. I hadn't made the wrong decision and toppled into the ravine, now had I? Without my head getting in the way, I'd performed a series of complex manoeuvres and arrived safely and precisely where I needed to be.

Right here. Right now.

MONTEREY DAYS
PIRATES DON'T GET ARRESTED

A journey is like marriage. The certain way to be wrong is to think you control it.

—JOHN STEINBECK

FOR THE NEXT WEEK I stayed in Palmillas, recovering from my self-imposed ordeal. Chon and Angel fussed like competing spouses, rebuilding my strength in double quick time with their superb cooking. Nata and his friends from the secondary school meanwhile shot a film for the Video Exchange Program and took photographs for the project that Theresa had started in Baja. I then saddled up the Raleigh and headed south towards Mazatlan, eager to track down Olly and Carole. But the note waiting for me at the post office contained disappointing news. Running low on funds, they'd had to return to Europe to find work.

I pressed on to Peru alone, working with youth groups along the way, everything from ragtag graffiti artists-cum-skateboarders in Mexico City to indigenous adobe-hut-dwelling Maya Quiche in the highlands of Guatemala, their village a day's walk from the nearest electricity to recharge camera batteries. In Guatemala City, the principal of a school plagued by gang violence merely pinned a good luck note to the outside of his locked office door. And in El Salvador, it took two blown tyres and a rambling detour into the hinterland of the San Miguel district to reach one UNESCO-affiliated establishment.

Incredibly, no cameras were damaged or stolen. The only setback occurred while soliciting Video Exchange volunteers at an all-girl's Catholic high school in Mexico City. By this point in the journey I'd completely forgotten about the salmon pink flutter dress at the bottom of one of my panniers, cushioning the spare video camera until it was needed to cross the Darien Gap. Addressing the entire school of some five hundred adolescent girls and assorted nuns and teachers, it was only after unravelling the bundle that I remembered. By which time it was too late, of course. The place had erupted, and I was as pink as the dress.

In Tegucigalpa, the capital of Honduras, more bad news was waiting. This time it was from Steve. He and Eilbhc had returned from

Ireland and were already in Quito, Ecuador, making arrangements for the Pacific crossing. The Ecuadorian Interior Ministry had recently issued a warning that 1997 would be one of the strongest El Niño years in history. Massive flood and storm surge damage was expected along the coast with roads like the Pan American closed by mudslides and washouts. Most worrying to the expedition was the National Oceanic and Atmospheric Administration (NOAA) prediction of a reversal of the prevailing anticlockwise surface currents in the Southeast Pacific.

This left us with two choices. Either we stayed in South America and risked being stranded for up to two years waiting for the anticlockwise pattern to reassert itself, or backtracked to San Francisco and tried to reach Australia by pedalling diagonally across the Pacific—the original less-favoured Plan B.

The Central American leg was duly aborted. A year had been lost and nearly five thousand miles travelled in the wrong direction.

FOR THE FIRST month of our journey south through the Americas, *Moksha* had been confined to a wire cage tucked out of sight behind the Monterey Maritime Museum. It took all of Stuart's accumulated charm and experience to lure prospective customers into what was effectively a sales trap, the price of freedom set at $20 for a tee shirt or name on the boat. Impressed by his dogged persistence, the museum's director, Donna Penwell, agreed to a more prominent location outside the main entrance, and from then on the punters stopped by in droves, fascinated by the strange yellow contraption surrounded by maps and information boards. Admission to the museum rose appreciably, along with the sale of merchandise to keep the expedition afloat.

Children were encouraged to liven up the inside of the central cabin with artwork and goodwill messages for the Pacific crossing. "Keep pedaling pussies. Pirates don't get arrested," read one morale booster, scribbled next to the drawing of a shark lunging out of a toilet bowl, about to sink its teeth into someone's backside. Stuart's explanation of over-the-side bathroom etiquette had obviously got a little lost in translation on that one.

It turned out the father of the five-year-old "Keep pedaling pussies" author was head of security at the nearby DoubleTree Hotel. Ian Satchell became the expedition's most dedicated local supporter, going so far as to volunteer his own two-room apartment as a temporary HQ. Steve and Eilbhe returned from Ecuador in September. I arrived soon after from Tegucigalpa, swelling the flat's occupancy to five.

We had one month to ready the boat for launch before the winter storms set in, and also develop an ecological footprints programme. Running concurrent to the voyage, schoolchildren from participating countries would examine the effects of human overconsumption on the health of the planet. Time, however, was against us. There just weren't enough hours in the day to have *Moksha* provisioned and the curriculum rolled out in time for an autumn departure.

A third option was proposed, one that didn't involve postponing the Pacific crossing or abandoning a field of learning that Steve and I believed crucial to help safeguard a sustainable future. Our breakthrough chat in the garden of the Bay View Boat Club a year earlier had declared that, "Anyone can cross an ocean by human power. Ordinary people *can* do extraordinary things." Why not really walk our talk and invite some new faces to pedal the first leg to Hawaii?

Casey Dunn, a congenial mop-headed Californian in his early twenties, was one of the Stanford students who'd redesigned *Moksha's* propulsion system. He teamed up with John Walker, an older, more cautious British naval officer studying Farsi at the Defense Language Institute. The men were both physically fit and extremely intelligent, more than capable of the task at hand, but destiny has a habit of imposing its own narrow agenda irrespective of the best-laid plans. Five days after departing Monterey Bay in near-perfect conditions, the wind strengthened to force 7 and the pair found themselves drifting on the sea anchor watching a steadily falling barometer. The low-pressure system predicted by meteorologists to amount to "little more than a light blow" was ramping up to be the first major gale of the winter storm season.

Disasters can nearly always be traced back to a single incident, without which other causative factors amount to nothing. For John and Casey, the genesis of their undoing was losing a blade off the wind generator. This was a minor glitch on its own: they had spare blades on board, and as soon as the weather improved and the boat stopped pitching and rolling, another one could have been fitted. But when the clouds moved in, rendering the solar panels ineffective, and John insisted they keep the navigation lights on at night for safety, their fate was sealed. The two gel batteries drained below the ten-volt minimum needed to maintain communications, and they opted to turn back. This was their second mistake. With a storm brewing, the prudent mariner heads away from land, not towards it.

After being battered continuously for two days, they glimpsed the saw-toothed coastline of Big Sur through the mist and rain. The handheld VHF had just enough power to put out a Mayday call. A helicopter was promptly scrambled from San Francisco to the north and a coastguard cutter launched from Morro Bay to the south.

Steve, Eilbhe, Stuart, and I raced down from Monterey and gathered in the brightly lit control room of the coastguard station. We were soon joined by Casey's grandfather, a grizzled ex-serviceman in his late sixties.

"I've been asked to come down here by the boy's mother," he growled by way of introduction. "Who, as you all know, is beside herself with worry. My priority is Casey's safe return."

The officer on duty gave the likely scenario: the chopper would get there first, winch John and Casey to safety, and abandon the boat.

"But if we lose her that'll be the end of the expedition!" protested Steve.

"That's no concern of the United States Coast Guard, sir," the officer replied curtly. "We're obliged to save life, not property."

Fair enough. But over the years *Moksha* had become a personality in her own right, as much a team member as any of us. Leaving her to smash against the cliffs was almost unthinkable. So, as we waited for news, the officer was plied with time-tested stories of the plucky little craft defying hell and high water on the Atlantic. And by the time the voice of the cutter skipper crackled over the radio, announcing they'd made better than expected headway and beaten the chopper to it, the officer was sufficiently moved to make a personal appeal to have *Moksha* towed off the rocks.

For the next twelve hours, it looked as if we'd lucked out. The lifeboat crew brought John and Casey safely to Morro Bay, leaving the boat tethered to a mooring buoy in the sheltered cove of San Simeon. Then fate dropped its other shoe. On the morning of December 4, the phone rang in Ian's apartment. It was the coastguard again. *Moksha* had capsized during the night and was slowly sinking.

SHE MADE FOR a pitiful sight, only her reddish belly visible between the breakers, centreboard wagging at us like an accusing finger. The only thing keeping the old girl from going under was a pocket of air trapped inside her wooden lungs.

The cheapest quote from a marine salvage company had come in at $30,000—a distant fantasy, given the mere $226 we had in the expedition checking account. The only option was to attempt an improvised recovery effort of our own. With discounts from rental shops prevailed upon by Stuart, we scrounged together essential equipment: sit-on-top kayaks, scuba tanks, a mask, regulator, and wetsuits.

Patience was another basic requirement. For two days the swell remained too high, and all we could do was stand on the pier and watch as *Moksha* wallowed like a moribund whale, tugging feebly at her mooring line. At night, the six of us—Steve, Eilbhe, Stuart, Casey, John, and I—huddled in sodden sleeping bags under beachside picnic tables, fantasizing of hot food. In our rush to leave Monterey, we'd left our tents behind as well as anything to cook with.

On the afternoon of the third day, the surf subsided enough to give it a go. Ian drove down from Monterey to lend a hand. As a former Navy SEAL, he had the most experience for this kind of thing—or so we hoped. We were sheltering out of the rain in the caretaker's boatshed when he sauntered in wearing a Stetson hat and cowboy boots. Was this "costume de rigueur" for naval salvage operations, we wondered?

"Okay, fellas." He flashed a toothy grin and pumped the air with his fists, a show of bravado to rally the troops. "Let's stick this pig!"

Stuart and Eilbhe stationed themselves on the end of the pier, ready to pass down fenders, buoys, and ropes. The rest of us launched the kayaks from the beach, punching through the surf zone and paddling the quarter mile to *Moksha.*

"Ian," Steve called out. "You still up for going underneath and having a look-see?"

The Special Forces sailor nodded, adjusted his regulator, and disappeared over the side of his kayak in a cloud of bubbles. The rest of us rafted up and waited. It was 4:05 pm, the sun already low in the west.

Ian reappeared, treading water beside Steve's boat. "Stoopid! Stoopid!" he spluttered. "This is *so* fucking dangerous. The lines from the wind generator are all tangled around the sea anchor rope, and a bunch of ration packs have burst open—it's impossible to see down there. But I'll try and clear as much wreckage as I can."

He disappeared again, resurfacing ten minutes later holding a dinner plate-sized portion of decking. The half-inch ply was still connected to one of the wind generator shrouds, explaining the mystery capsize. Instead of securing the mooring line through the eyebolt in the bow stem, the lifeboat crew had tied it around the much flimsier forward shroud. The seesaw action of the fully laden boat had torn out the section of underlying timber, allowing seawater to flood the Rathole and the central cabin. With two out of three compartments swamped, it was only a matter of time before *Moksha* lost buoyancy and turned turtle.

Having done his part, Ian headed for land to be back in time for his night shift. The rest of us tethered our kayaks to *Moksha's* upturned rudder before slipping into the water.

"Ooof!" John grimaced. "It's effin' cold."

Fed by the California Current sweeping south from Alaska, the water off the western seaboard of the US seldom reaches above ten degrees Celsius in winter. Wetsuits certainly helped, except that I'd somehow ended up with a sleeveless one designed for summer temperatures.

"Okay, everyone," hollered Steve, his eyes blinking against the cold. "Let's see if we can pull her over."

While I swam to the opposite side, ready to act as a counterbalance, Steve, John, and Casey clambered onto the starboard gunwale and grabbed the top of the centreboard. Pushing and pulling as one, we built the momentum back and forth. On the tenth pull, the hull kept rolling, dumping everyone back in the water. *Moksha* hovered perpendicular, teetering like a drunk, then continued to roll through three hundred and sixty degrees back to her former belly-up posture. A moment later, propelled like a slingshot, the fifty-pound wind generator head cannoned into the water beside Casey.

"That was close!" he grinned.

We were back where we started. Only now *Moksha* was even lower in the water, having lost precious air during her orbit.

"She's too unstable," said John, shaking his head. "Probably a load of waterlogged food and gear lying on her roof."

We tried again, this time securing a large orange fender to the port beam, positive buoyancy to prevent another full rotation. It was no use. *Moksha* hesitated a little longer before rolling back the way she'd come.

"All we're doing is losing more of the air pocket!" I cried in frustration.

The situation was looking desperate. Only a few inches of boat remained above water, over which successive waves lapped with alarming ease. Our pride and joy, the symbol of our hopes, dreams, and 10,000 miles of blood, sweat, and tears from Greenwich was hanging on by a thread.

As if drawing down the final curtain, the sun sank below the horizon, taking with it the last of the heat and the light. We'd been in the freezing water for well over an hour, and having drawn the short straw on wetsuits, I was shivering uncontrollably. When I said something about the light fading fast, I realized I was slurring with hypothermia.

"Let's call it a day." Steve sighed in resignation. "Try something else in the morning."

But we all knew *Moksha* wouldn't be there in the morning.

"Hold on," said Casey, his teeth chattering. "I've got an idea. If I crack Ian's spare tank in the forward compartment and seal the bulkhead behind it, the air might displace enough water for her to stay upright."

We had nothing to lose. Grabbing the scuba gear, Casey slipped underwater, pulling the spare cylinder with him. A minute later he was back, tank in place. The four of us took up positions on either side of the hull.

At first, nothing happened. *Moksha* continued to flounder like a whale in its death throes, emitting deep, sonorous groans as her watery bowels filled with gas. Then, little by little, she began to rise. One inch … two inches … three inches …

Steve's face was almost completely shrouded in darkness. "Now!" he yelled.

The boat came easily, righting with a great swoosh of water cascading off her decks. Arriving at the upright position, she wavered for several seconds, fighting for balance like a newborn foal. While the rest of us braced the gunwales, Steve shinnied into the cockpit with a bucket and began to bail furiously.

SPLATCH ... SPLATCH ... SPLATCH ...

Next John levered himself aboard. "Let's have a go with that, Steve," he hissed. "I'm bloody freezing."

After fifteen minutes of hard bailing, the water level had dropped sufficiently to use the bilge pump. All four of us were now huddled around the hatch, taking turns pumping or bailing to stave off hypothermia. I peered at the ghostly white faces around me. They looked exhausted, drawn, and impossibly cold. But there was something else: the unmistakable glimmer of triumph. We'd done it. We'd beaten the odds, snatching the dream from the jaws of catastrophe. We'd resurrected *Moksha*.

IN TRUTH, IT wasn't a full resurrection. All we managed to bring back that pivotal day at San Simeon was a weak but vital pulse. It took nearly a year to nurse *Moksha* back to full health. First, her guts had to be ripped out and the hull sanded down to bare wood for a complete repaint inside and out. Then all the fittings and equipment needed to be replaced—electronics, wiring, solar panels, wind generator, radio, lifejackets, life rafts, Inmarsat-C system, laptop, stove, utensils, and provisions—in all, tens of thousands of dollars' worth of gear.

Steve based himself at Fort Baker on the north side of the Golden Gate Bridge, restoring *Moksha* by day and sleeping in an old van parked behind the yacht club at night. I stayed with Shirley in Bernal Heights and worked the computers and phones. Sponsorship proposals were resubmitted to marine suppliers, and what couldn't be cajoled with promises of product exposure had to be paid for in hard cash earned through speaking. It was months and months of the same old grind, like in London, Miami, Colorado, San Francisco, Monterey, and now San Francisco again. For every hour of human-powered travel, it was taking three hours of fundraising to pay for it.

One step forward, one step back, seemed to be the new status quo. Two attempts to cross the Pacific had so far failed: the first, by way of Peru, stymied by El Niño; the second, via Hawaii, unhinged by a ten-dollar wind generator blade. Three years after Steve and Eilbhe first rolled into San Francisco, the expedition hadn't progressed any nearer towards Greenwich.

THE PACIFIC
PEDALLING TO HAWAII

If you are a brave man, you will do nothing: if you are fearful you may do much, for none but cowards have need to prove their bravery.

—APSLEY CHERRY-GARRARD, *The Worst Journey in the World*

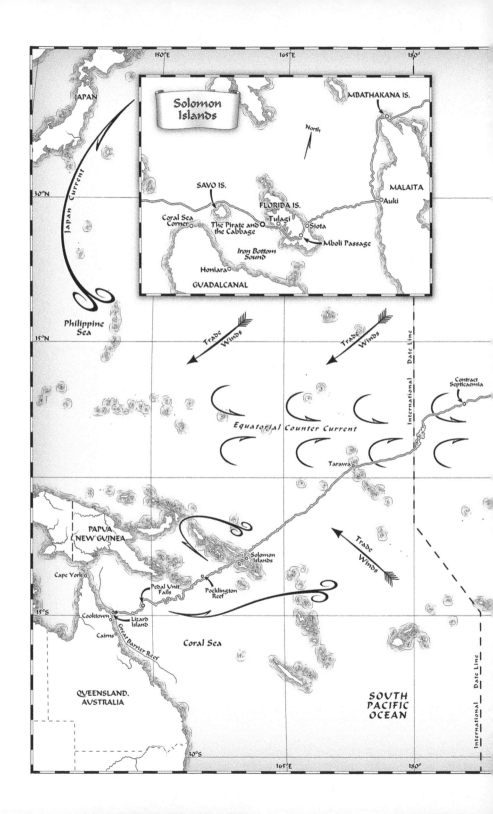

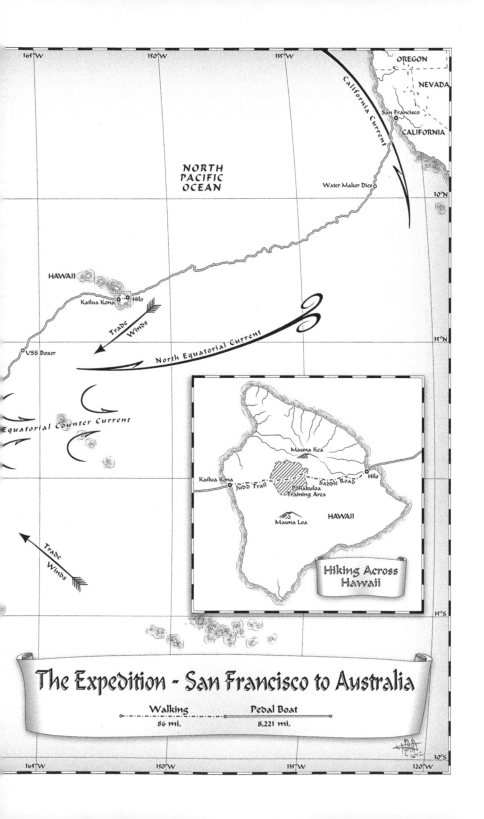

The Expedition - San Francisco to Australia

September 20, 1998

"**K**ENNY, YOU'RE LOOKING WELL, mate."
I was lying. He looked like crap. At least compared to
the last time I'd seen him, two years before in Colorado. As well as a bandaged foot, he'd put on weight and was chain smoking. The proboscis was gone along with a certain youthful vitality. He seemed hardened, more cynical.

"How're things?" I continued.

"Nae sae bad, an' you?"

"Oh, you know, the usual."

"Chaos, then?"

I smiled. "Exactly. Getting the boat ready never seems to get any easier or the to do lists any shorter."

In May, Steve and I had agreed to something unimaginable a year previously: pedal together to Hawaii. Five months on, *Moksha's* refit complete, we found ourselves on the eve of another departure. The extended expedition family had assembled in the Presidio Yacht Club to rally round and help with final preparations.

"So which part of the world have you just come from, Ken?"

"Kosovo."

"Working for the BBC?"

He nodded, taking a drag on his cigarette.

"What happened to your leg?"

"Some bastard shot at me runnin' across a field in Macedonia. Broke mah ankle."

"Jesus."

"Noo, a Serb. It's jist a hairline fracture, tho. Should be back tae wark in a couple ay weeks. It's guid tae see you 'n Steve pedallin' again. How did tha' happen?"

I thought of El Niño, and of John and Casey's ordeal. "Well, when Mother Nature kicks you in the arse enough times, it's time to start taking her more seriously."

There were other reasons, of course. John and Casey had their own lives to get on with and couldn't wait the eleven months for *Moksha* to be refurbished. Steve and I had also mellowed—attitudes softened, angers assuaged, especially in light of *Moksha's* near sinking. In one of those strange but reassuring paradoxes, the act of relinquishing the dream had somehow brought us back together.

Moreover, the Ecological Footprints Program was now in place. Fleets of school buses had been arriving at Fort Baker for over a fortnight, emitting a stream of jabbering fourth, fifth, and sixth graders for half-day orientations. Each class took turns at four learning stations. Steve explained how *Moksha* worked: the pedal system, solar panels, wind generator, and so forth. Shirley and Stuart screened a documentary that Kenny had recently sold to Discovery Channel. Suzanne Geller, a local fifth-grade teacher and contributor to the footprints curriculum, taught latitude and longitude. I demonstrated safety and communications equipment, including the ruggedized laptop we'd be using to keep in email contact with students during the voyage.

"Reit," said Kenny, hobbling away. "Better go fix that microphone tae th' waterproof camera hoosin'. Seeya in a bit."

The launch party was already in full swing upstairs. JimBo Trout and the Fishpeople were working their bluegrass magic, and grog flowed in abundance. I tracked Steve down to run through final preparations. In less than twelve hours we'd be striking out into the Pacific together, with 2,400 very empty miles separating us from Hawaii.

We heard a cough and turned to see *Moksha's* propeller maker, Scott Morrison, clutching the pedal unit and grinning sheepishly. He'd been down at the wharf giving the propulsion system a final once-over. He tilted the unit upside down, and seawater streamed from a series of perforations along its length.

Steve and I looked at each other in disbelief.

"Electrolysis," Scott explained. "From the boats in the marina."

It was another painful lesson, this time how different metals produce a battery effect when immersed in a positively charged hydrous environment, such as a harbour or marina. Weaker metals dissolve, robbed of their ions through chemical decomposition. Without a sacrificial zinc anode attached, the thin alloy casing of the pedal unit had been eaten away in less than a week.

"Un-fucking-believable," I cursed under my breath. "What do we do now?"

"Get the beers in, obviously," said Steve, smiling wryly.

One week later

SHARDS OF SPANGLED sunlight ricocheted off a modest chop as the Golden Gate Bridge shrank to miniature in *Moksha's* wake. A seagull shrieked at us, and the green, velveteen fingers of the Marin headlands tapered into the water off our starboard beam. Gradually, almost imperceptibly, the North American continent slipped beneath the waves.

"How do you feel, Stevie?"

Sweat poured off my crewmate as he toiled at the pedals. "Remarkably ordinary," he smiled. "Like it's just a normal day. I don't have any of that knotted tension like when we left on the Atlantic." The radio suddenly crackled to life: *Formosa Eight. Formosa Eight. Pilot boat San Francisco. Channel sixteen.*

"Why do you think it's easier this time?" I asked.

Steve thought for a moment. "So much has changed in four years. I wish I could have been who I am now when we left Portugal, but that's not possible, of course. It's all part of the process."

It had been a frantic week since Scott's chance discovery. While a replacement pedal unit was rushed from the factory in Michigan, all the provisions had to be disinterred from *Moksha's* fore and aft compart-

ments, allowing her to be pulled from the water. The stainless steel propulsion box was then lathered in anti-corrosive paint and zinc anodes
attached. Racing against the clock to make the next favourable tide,
Moksha was back in the water and ready to go in time for us to catch last
orders at the TWO AM CLUB in Sausalito.

Three hours into the voyage, we switched—for me an act of small
mercy. The distraction of pedalling would help ward off seasickness
and the mother of all hangovers kicking in. Steve slumped on the passenger seat, braced himself between the oars, and let his head loll like a
pendulum in time with the swell.

"Bloody stupid habit really, isn't it," I remarked, grabbing the steering toggles and pressing my feet to the pedals.

Of the two of us, Steve had been slightly more sensible, leaving the
bar at midnight to finish bagging the ingredients to make fresh bread
on the voyage. Even so, he was suffering. He raised his head and threw
me a bloodshot look. "What is?" he grunted.

"Getting rat-arsed before going to sea."

He nodded limply. "Hmm, right. Got to stick to tradition, though.
This is the big one, remember?"

The Pacific, covering a third of the planet, was always going to be
the biggest geographical hurdle facing a human-powered circumnavigation. If we missed Hawaii, next stop was the tiny island atoll of Tarawa, 2,500 miles to the southwest. Miss both and it was a further 2,600
miles to Australia, making for a very long voyage indeed—up to a year
on the water.

The support boat, *Penelope*, made one last pass for Kenny to get his
parting shot, then left us to it. Released from media duties, Steve curled
up on the passenger seat in his yellow sou'wester and tried to sleep.
Stretching out full length was impossible. The Rathole was jammed
with items thrown in at the last minute: bags of fruits and vegetables,
a loaf of bread, laptop, power cables, toilet bags, and a blow-up sheep
called Dolly.

After turning the bow to 220 degrees, I fished through the ceiling netting for my ocean ring. My friend from Pueblo, Cynthia Ramu, whose art students had painted a mural of *Moksha* on the Arkansas River levee, pressed it into my hand the morning April and I set out for the West Coast. "A good luck charm," she promised, "for the Pacific."

The ring was beautiful, silver cresting waves etched in a never-ending wheel. I slipped it on my ring finger and made a pledge to the sea: *From now on, we are one.*

Superstition usually left me cold, but John and Casey's experience had served to remind me how an ocean is never conquered, only indulged long enough to pass. Every minute of every hour conning across the fathomless deep was time borrowed from a cache of ever-decreasing odds set against the mariner. By wedding myself to the sea, I would become privy to her shifting moods and elaborate idiosyncrasies, bettering our chances of survival. At least this was my theory: to navigate the tempestuous waters with the same acuity of seamanship conducive to harmonious matrimony on land. And sure enough, in due course the ring became as indispensible to me as charts or weather forecasts, a reminder to listen to the ocean and her breath, to the quickening or slowing of its cadence, and to watch for the creasing of her countenance as she angered—complexion darkening, spittle streaking—preparing to strike.

Steve awoke suddenly. "Woaah! What's going on?" He twisted his head at me. "Where am I?"

"It's okay," I said calmly.

He clawed himself upright, bug-eyed with sleep. "That was weird. I dreamt I was on a boat that had slipped its moorings and was drifting out to sea."

"You are, mate."

Chuckling, we made ready to switch positions. A manoeuvre that had become second nature on the Atlantic was once again awkward and ungainly. Handholds were missed, heads and shoulders crunched. The serrated teeth of the pedals savaged our shins as we wrestled past. And in case we'd forgotten how good we'd had it on land, a wave flopped over the side and drenched us both.

"Ah, yes," muttered Steve, using a free hand to squeegee the water off his face. "It's all coming back to me now."

Those first 24 hours back on board were always going to be a brutal transition, being biffed, bashed, pinched, pummelled, soaked and scalded by the sadistic whims of a capricious universe. The seasickness continued, sapping every ounce of enthusiasm. Disappearing over the side became an increasingly attractive option, limited as we were to pedalling, throwing up, nibbling on crackers smeared with Marmite, then pedalling and throwing up some more.

The night of September 28 was black as pitch, the sliver of new moon eclipsed by a swab of dense cloud. The trick to staving off seasickness in the dark was to concentrate on the red degree markers around the compass—210° … 220° … back to 210°—and listening to music. As *Moksha* responded to each peristaltic wave, lunging and reeling as if massaged through the intestines of some labyrinthine sea creature, I slipped on the headphones for a dose of Creedence Clearwater Revival.

The second morning broke cold and damp, the sky a cheerless flannel of steel. Cunning little waves made dashes for the hatch and barged in unannounced. The ocean beneath hardened to the colour of ink, and a landless horizon surfaced on all sides. We were easing away from the coastal shallows and into deeper water.

As we neared the Farallon Islands, movement off the starboard beam caught my eye, an instinctively familiar shape breaking the play of light on water.

"Stop pedalling, Stevie."

"What is it?"

"Shark."

The creature slid effortlessly by, waving its dorsal fin at us. Steve pedalled backwards to get a closer look.

"Don't run it over and piss it off," I laughed nervously.

"Wow," whispered Steve. "It's massive, isn't it?"

We were in the aptly named Red Triangle, a region extending west of the San Francisco peninsula responsible for forty per cent of all great white shark attacks in US waters. The predators were drawn to the abundance of food in the area: seals, sea otters, and sea lions. Occasionally, a swimmer or surfer got caught in the mix.

"That," I declared, pointing at the receding fin, "is one very good reason I will *not* be swimming today."

Other pelagics paid us visits. A pod of dolphins appeared at dusk, chasing each other's phosphorescent tails with the choreographed grace of underwater comets. And the following day a pair of finback whales breached upwind, covering *Moksha* in a fine drizzle of whale slobber and filling the air with a fishy stench that turned our already fragile stomachs.

October 5

LIKE SLIPPING INTO an old pair of shoes, former routines and habits became natural again after a week at sea: sponging water from the bottom of the boat, hooking sunglasses in the port side netting so they wouldn't get scratched or broken, and placing a chock of wood behind the pedal seat to compensate for my shorter legs. We were also anticipating the waves better, bracing each time we heard a telltale hiss.

In most other respects, however, the voyage was turning out quite different to the Atlantic. No rigid pedal shifts were set in place this time. Instead of an unsparing two hours on, two hours off, day after day until land was reached, we tailored the schedule according to how we felt. If one of us complained of fatigue and needed more sleep, the other would pedal longer. The courtesy would soon be returned—what went around came around quickly on Planet *Moksha*. Trust replaced suspicion, cooperation competition. We treated each other with consideration and respect, greeting moodiness with compassion rather than frigid detachment.

"I don't think we realized how stressful it was on the first crossing," Steve commented on the morning of the eighth day. "I know I was anxious. Scared, too. I remember thinking: *I might as well go numb, not deal, just to get through this.*"

I was cooking breakfast while he pedalled. Not from out-of-date army rations this crossing, but a selection of freeze-dried meals sold by a company specializing in high-tech nutritional foods. In spite of the hype, most of it was vile, especially the primavera entrée indistinguishable from liquid cement. The only palatable meal was porridge, impossible for even the most cack-handed food producer to botch.

"I wish you could have told me that at the time," I said. "I thought you were being arrogant."

Steve looked taken aback. "Arrogant, really?"

The oatmeal thickened to a glutinous roil, air bubbles forcing themselves through the gravelly muck before popping like blisters, rendering the surface a cratered, lunar landscape.

"Well, it was hard to tell you anything," he countered. "You pretty much cut me off."

It was true. The pursuit of enlightenment on the Atlantic had made me selfish, a bad team player, forcing us to pedal two separate voyages by the end. But spiritual inquiry, by definition, calls for isolation to nurture the stillness of mind needed to release the power of the subconscious. The seeker typically eschews family and friends, often incurring the disapproval of non-seekers who perceive only worthless self-absorption. In this way, cultivating One Pointed Attention on the voyage had involved turning my attention inward, away from external distractions, Steve included.

I admitted as much and made another confession: "I was still angry at you. Angry at how you treated Chris and Hugo, and how you took decisions back then—single-minded, totally driven. The expedition was your baby, but I missed our old friendship, when neither of us was in charge. Being on the expedition was like the army again. So when you were down in the dumps, I thought: *fuck him if he can't handle it.* Can't say I'm proud of that now, but that's just the way it was." I paused for a moment. "This voyage is another story, though."

Mollified by the disclosure, Steve's expression softened. "How so?"

"We're communicating, for one. And you?"

My partner looked out through the Perspex to the rolling blue horizon. The clouds to the north showed signs of lifting, a ribbon of pink heralding the first break in the weather for days.

"Just not having any assigned roles or schedules, I think. Crossing from Portugal, the routine was so regimented it allowed us to cut ourselves off from each other. The fact that we had two hours on, two hours off, meant we never had to ask the question, 'How do you feel?' It didn't matter, because you had to go on, and that's all there was to it."

I smiled, remembering something. "Like this morning when you had an extra hour in the Rathole. If it were the Atlantic, I'd have been banging a saucepan next to your head after the first minute!"

We shook our heads at the ridiculousness of what was now, thankfully, a bygone era, relieved that our friendship was back on track. Aside from the time we'd smoked a joint, conversation like this would have been inconceivable on our maiden voyage.

I pulled the porridge off the new alcohol burning stove and doled it out, remembering to add an extra spoonful to Steve's bowl. This was one formality that hadn't changed. To avoid even the slightest chance of mistrust, meals were still divvied up on the bottom of the boat in full view of the other person. I was about to pass Steve his when I heard a low, rolling hiss. The incoming wave slammed into the starboard beam, pitching *Moksha* to port and shoving me against the side of the cabin. I looked up in time to see a crescent of water curl gracefully through the hatch and land with a self-congratulatory FLOP! in our porridge bowls.

Steve and I stared at each other for a few seconds, and then burst out laughing. Washing out the spoiled porridge, I started all over again.

THE PRIMARY WATERMAKER died on the morning of the fourteenth day. Steve pulled the reserve unit from the grab bag and began lashing it to the starboard side oar.

Thank goodness for the backup, I thought.

He tied off the last knot, threw the intake hose over the side, and started pumping the little black handle. Designed for life rafts, the device produced only a quarter of what the primary unit once did. It would now take up to six hours of pumping each day in addition to the pedal shifts to meet our basic drinking needs.

"Bit Mickey Mouse, isn't it," I said, picking up the video camera and pressing record. "Like something out of a Christmas cracker."

A procession of bubbles migrated slowly along the output hose, at the end of which a single drop of water formed, hovered, and then fell. It was several seconds before another appeared. Steve reached for the red petrol can we used for a water container. "That's as fast as it'll go," he said for the camera, "all the way to Hawaii. But hey, at least it works."

Next morning, I awoke to the sound of clattering pots and pans and rain drumming on the roof of the Rathole. I watched as Steve scrambled out on deck and secured the hastily gathered cookware with bungee cords. He then stripped off and embraced the sky. Freshwater showers were rare privileges aboard *Moksha*. Apart from an occasional washcloth steamed in the pressure cooker, life on the briny was an exclusively salty affair.

The squall passed. Steve poured the contents of each pan into the red container, before repositioning them in the bilges where a hose ran from the gunwales—*Moksha's* superstructure was designed with rainwater collection in mind. Reaching under one of the compartment covers, he flipped a stopcock, releasing a mini-deluge.

"Bit salty," he murmured, tasting it with an index finger. "Okay for cooking, though."

The backup watermaker died that afternoon. None of the wrenches in the tool bag were big enough to unscrew the cylinder cap to see if it could be fixed. This left us with twelve gallons of emergency fresh water stored in canvas bags, a gallon of harvested rainwater, and a little less of brackish. Watching the last drops fall from the output hose, my tongue turned stirrup-leather-dry.

"We could flag down a ship?" Steve suggested hopefully.

His optimism, though well intentioned, I found irritating. "Oh yeah, and what if we don't see one?"

All morning I'd been trying to mend the primary pump: taking the casing apart, reseating the seals, before carefully reassembling. Each time I tried the handle, hoping to feel pressure, nothing happened—the only pressure I was building was my own. I recalled with rising trepidation the experience of running out of water on Isla Tiburon and Cerro del Muerto in Mexico. The backup pump failing put me over the edge.

"Useless piece of fucking shite!" I fumed, reaching for the claw hammer to bash the thing out of existence. "Why don't these people check to make sure their stuff works properly before it leaves the factory? I mean *really*. Especially when lives are at stake."

"Jason, don't!"

I hesitated, hammer poised midair. Steve was right. We needed everything, even the broken watermakers. Parts from one could be cannibalized to fix the other.

My father read about our water crisis in the daily blog. At the start of the expedition, my parents had been lukewarm to the whole enterprise (and who could blame them after our laughable sea trials in Devon). But years of vicarious living through umpteen setbacks—the shattered legs in Colorado, the dead-end miles to Peru, the interminable lack of funding—had convinced them this wasn't just another wild prank, fated to fizzle. Now my father, with whom I'd never really seen eye to eye, was providing logistics support for the Pacific. It was another of those serendipitous twists on the itinerant path, one that had taken me far from home and family, leading to reconciliation with my father. And there was an added bonus. Being flesh and blood, he would do whatever it took to get his son out of a tight spot.

I almost choked when I read his email the next morning. "Listen to this," I said to Steve. "My dad's been in contact with US Naval Command. There's a destroyer in our area, apparently. All he needs is our coordinates, and they'll try and deliver us a replacement watermaker."

Steve grinned. "Good old Sebert!"

I wrinkled my nose. "It's a bit much, though, isn't it?"

"'Tis a bit. We're not exactly at death's door. Better not bother the Pentagon just yet."

A week later, with only four gallons of drinking water remaining and our situation looking dire, Steve discovered a way, albeit accidently, to unscrew the cap off the reserve watermaker. There was nothing on board he hated more than the articulated "magic arm" clamp that Kenny had supplied us with to film from different camera angles. When, for the third time that morning, he conked his head on it, I saw with fresh eyes how wide its jaws were.

"I'm gonna throw that bloody thing overboard *right now,*" Steve vowed, rubbing his head painfully and removing the clamp.

"Don't do it," I said.

The pump was disassembled in a jiffy and the culprit, a loose hose clamp, reattached. Fresh water began flowing a few seconds later, transforming Steve's troubled relationship with the magic arm.

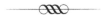

"How do you kill a blonde?" Steve asked, reading as he pedalled.

"No idea."

"Put a scratch and sniff sticker on the bottom of a swimming pool."

I winced. "How old are these kids again?"

As the afternoon heat tapered to a blissful deliverance of cool, we observed certain rituals: boiling the kettle for tea, carving a notch in the cabin timbers to mark off another day, and opening a letter from one of the classrooms following the voyage. The brightly coloured envelopes contained jokes and cartoons to keep us smiling and laughing (or, like today, groaning). Email worked well enough via the new Inmarsat-C data terminal, but when it came to a more meaningful connection, handwritten messages were hard to beat.

Indeed, the introduction of technology into the expedition had come at a hidden price. Computers, satellite phones, and the Internet supplied a real-time link with students unimaginable even a year previously, allowing them to travel the world virtually with us, but wilderness immersion was now a distant memory. No more contemplating sunsets, absorbed in the moment. We contemplated a flickering screen, describing the sunsets instead.

Steve tucked the joke into an envelope marked Day 22 in large orange and purple letters and grabbed the video camera. "So what lesson activity are we on today, Jase?"

Our Ecological Footprints Program was entering its fourth week. While Steve filmed, I began sorting a week's worth of our refuse into three categories—biodegradable, non-biodegradable, and reusable—before weighing each in turn using a set of fish scales. Biodegradable waste went over the side. Reusable items, like the food container lids that doubled as barnacle scrapers, remained aboard. Inorganic plastics and metals were set aside to recycle once we reached Hawaii.

Students would be doing the same assignment, only sorting their waste at home and in the classroom rather than inside a boat. Each group, *Moksha* included, would then email their weekly data to the webmaster for posting online. More than three hundred teams from five countries were taking part, represented by icons in the shape of human footprints. As data accumulated, the size of the footprints grew proportionately, allowing interpretation, comparison, and contrast.*

To illustrate the far-reaching effects of human consumption, we'd chosen seven footprint areas: food, water, energy, living space, materials and goods, waste and pollution, and travel and transport. As Steve's overview explained: *Everywhere we go, and in everything we do, we leave an impression, an effect, like footprints on the beach. Each time we eat a meal, take a shower, go to school, play sports, buy a new pair of shoes, everything we do changes our physical world just a tiny little bit.*

Studying geography and biology together at London University, Steve and I shared a common interest in humans, the societies they create, and the natural world that ultimately sustains both. Geography shed light on the interaction between populations and their supporting environments. Biology, in particular its evolutionary arm, looked at the development of the human brain, the emerging science of consciousness, and the ability of *Homo sapiens* to live within finite means.

The story of Rapa Nui in the South Pacific offered a case in point. Famous for its hand-hewn statues, the sixty-six-square-mile island once supported a human population of some 20,000 inhabitants whose

---

* We borrowed the programme title from *Our Ecological Footprint*, a seminal guide for reducing human impact on Earth by authors Mathis Wackernagel and William Rees.

Polynesian ancestors originally arrived by outrigger canoe. Within just a few hundred years, however, only 111 people remained. So what happened?

Unearthing the evidence, archaeologists believe an ecological crash brought about by the islanders themselves principally to blame. By the time the Dutch explorer Jacob Roggeveen made landfall in 1722, all the native trees had been felled to transport and erect bigger and more impressive moai, the socio-religious monuments used by the chiefs to lend credence to their authority. Massive soil degradation and erosion followed, causing widespread crop failures. The means to build canoes for fishing was also compromised. As starvation and famine took hold, competition for protein and other vital resources played out as a nightmarish descent into social chaos, civil war, and eventually cannibalism. "Your grandmother's flesh sticks in my teeth" is an insult used by the people of Rapa Nui even to this day.

What made the story so compelling was the chilling parallel to human colonization of Earth. Just as pre-twentieth-century Rapa Nui was an island isolated by water, making it impossible for food and provisions to be brought in, or inhabitants be taken off to relieve population pressure, so the planet we live on is an island isolated by space. Which begs the obvious question: does Rapa Nui offer a glimpse into the fate of humankind, with multinational corporations playing the parts of paramount chiefs competing for dwindling resources?

In our ecological footprint experiments, *Moksha* served as a form of scientific control. The boat was effectively a closed system, a laboratory setting in which Steve and I were the rats. A thousand miles from land, there was little chance of resupply, and if our provisions ran out, neither of us could easily jump ship. Solar panels and the wind turbine generated electricity, seawater was filtered to produce drinking water, and transportation came from our own muscles. We could grow sprouts and catch fish, but unless we managed our resources responsibly, life aboard could get ugly pretty quickly.

Who would eat whom first became the running joke.

The bigger picture wasn't a joke at all, of course. The near extinction of humans on Rapa Nui became a powerful metaphor in class discussions on sustainability and a habitable planet for future generations. Would the doomed islanders have chosen a different fate for themselves if they'd known what was in store by chopping down the last tree? Not if present-day attitudes were anything to go by. In spite of incontrovertible proof of man-induced climate change, species extinctions, and biodiversity decline, as well as a wealth of information on how to live more simply, people still behaved like the good times would last forever. Joseph Conrad's damning verdict on the human condition appeared to be correct: "To tear treasure out of the bowels of the land was their desire, with no more moral purpose at the back of it than there is in burglars breaking into a safe."*

Is there hope? For children, saddled with the fate of the world, there has to be. Calling attention to *Moksha's* predictably small footprint wasn't the primary aim of the curriculum. Nor was it to embarrass anyone from richer, more extravagant societies. We merely hoped to inspire in students what we believed to be the most effective tool in preventing a Rapa Nui-style outcome on a global scale:

A questioning mind.

Critical Eye asks: What are my real needs versus perceived needs? How will my lifestyle choices affect my children, grandchildren, and great grandchildren? Does it even matter if the human species becomes extinct? If so, what can I, in my own sphere of influence, do about it?

BY DAY TWENTY-NINE, we'd reached the halfway point. The backup watermaker was still producing, but we were down to our third and final pedal unit. Equipment breakdowns were to be expected on a long-haul

---

* *Heart of Darkness.*

voyage: the saltwater environment was harsh and unforgiving, especially on metal and electronics, and we spent countless hours disassembling hardware between teetering knees, balancing screws, nuts, and washers in our laps. Corrosion was kept in check using wire brushes and emery paper, then greased to arrest further decay. Nevertheless, the last piece of gear we expected to fail considering how much time and effort had been spent overhauling it was the propulsion system.

"Come on, big boy," Steve said gently, stroking the unit like a thoroughbred racehorse. "You're our last chance."

"Twelve hundred miles to go," I added encouragingly. "You can do it!"

Steve kissed the metal collar where Scott had inscribed the epithet: THE DOG'S BOLLOCKS. "Yeah, we wanted to save the best till last, see?"

Unable to afford a customized drive, we'd settled on a unit designed for recreational craft traversing rivers and lakes. The propeller shafts, despite having been beefed up for our purposes, were the still weakest link. The forces involved in powering a 4,000-pound mass across thousands of miles of turbulent ocean were simply too great.

Steve fitted the propeller and zinc anode to the new shaft, reattached the crank arms, and guided the unit through the stainless steel box into the water, before fastening down the latches with four loud snaps. Lastly, he replaced the screwdriver, two crescent wrenches, and an assortment of Allen keys in the tool bag and wiped the filth from his hands with an old tee shirt.

"Fingers crossed," I said.

Steve nodded. "And everything else."

Arranging a sweat-encrusted towel under his naked buttocks, my crewmate slid the pedal seat back into position and made a few tentative rotations. The unit turned effortlessly, barely making a sound. But it wouldn't be quiet for long.

AFTER A MONTH and a half at sea, we crossed the Tropic of Cancer: latitude N23°26'. The ocean was now crystalline, revealing an array of exotic animals easing their way through the void. A magnificent purple and gold turtle as wide as a manhole cover paddled by, and what I briefly mistook for a translucent butterfly balancing precariously on the water revealed itself to be the sail of a juvenile Portuguese Man of War, its lethal tentacles barely formed.

Seven hundred miles east of Hawaii, the trade winds blew a steady ten to fifteen knots from the northeast, and the sky remained fathomless blue for days on end, interrupted only by scattered bands of polka dot clouds. The conditions were perfect, our progress stellar; sixty-mile days weren't uncommon. Aside from a squall blustering through every now and then, the personality of the Pacific was proving to be noticeably more refined than that of her boorish Atlantic cousin.

All this translated to maintaining favourable relations between Steve and me. So far we'd had only one argument, a brief one over a missing packet of M&Ms (it turned out they'd fallen into one of the food bins). Otherwise, the crossing was like chalk and cheese to the first. For his part, Steve had approached going to sea very differently this time, devising coping strategies before leaving San Francisco. These were designed to take his mind off the destination, Hawaii, and foster involvement with daily life aboard.

Bringing along a bundle of Fabulous Furry Freak Brothers comics was one (heavyweight books, on the other hand, especially any related to the field of cognitive science, were banned). Getting creative in the kitchen was another. We'd brought wheat, alfalfa, and sesame seeds to germinate in glass jars. Every day we rinsed the seedlings with a tablespoon of fresh water, and after a week full-grown sprouts were ready to harvest. Munching on a handful of fresh greens long after the surviving vegetables had gone mouldy gave us a tremendous psychological boost.*

Steve also made fresh bread, a welcome supplement to the freeze-dried meals that remained stubbornly inedible, even with our best efforts to resuscitate them with spices. "They've got a nerve," he muttered darkly every time pasta primavera came on the menu, "calling this stuff *gourmet.*"

First, he would add a cup of seawater and two cups of fresh water to a Ziploc bag pre-mixed with flour, yeast, seeds, and diced nuts. After kneading thoroughly, the doughy clump was transferred to a metal bowl and steamed inside the pressure cooker for half an hour. The result was a volleyball-sized dumpling, pallid as a corpse and lightly sweating. On land you'd think twice about putting any of it in your mouth, but at sea, with our appetites raging, it was the most delectable, lip-smacking bread either of us had ever tasted. Especially toasted. One of the highlights of the voyage was taking a break midway through a graveyard shift to heat a slice over the stove, and then lathering it in apricot jam before inhaling.

And yet, in spite of all his attempts to make the voyage more bearable, Steve often seemed elsewhere.

"I've been thinking a lot about home recently," he announced one morning, "and where it is. The road? England?"

He was bleary-eyed having woken from an hour of fitful sleep snatched on a square of canvas suspended across the central cabin. When the Creeping Grey Funk reared its ugly head and both of us needed to rest, the Bouncy Castle, as it became known, offered a preferred alternative to the stern compartment with its bags of stinking rubbish. That said, it was called the Bouncy Castle for a reason. With no way to brace oneself against the violent rocking motion of the boat, the makeshift hammock had all the trappings of a rolling torture machine.

---

* A boost to our health, too. Packed with vitamins A, B, C, E, and K, sprouts are also high in antioxidants, calcium, carotene, chlorophyll, iron, lecithin, magnesium, niacin, pantothenic acid, phosphorus, potassium, zinc, amino acids, and protein.

I, too, had just stirred, except from four hours of luxurious, uninter-
rupted sleep in the Rathole. Feeling suitably rested, my perspective on
life was entirely altered. It was like being on a different boat, on a different ocean. "Do you think you could ever fully adapt to being out here?"
I asked, swinging my legs out and shuffling into my sandals.

Steve was swaddled in his sleeping bag like a cocooned larva, rolling
in time with the swell. Shifting onto his elbows, he rubbed his eyes with
the heels of his hands, and replied, "I dunno. Maybe there's just not
enough that I really enjoy doing on the boat. I like standing in the hatch
at sunrise, having a cup of coffee and a packet of M&Ms, going for a
swim—the momentary escapes from the daily grind."

"Would you rather be in an office?"

"God, no! But I'm pretty sure I'll never get to the point where I'm
indifferent about seeing land again and content to just be here. I'll always be a bit"—he lifted his gaze, searching for the words above my
head—"somewhere else, if I'm completely honest. It's so claustropho-
bic and unnatural, restricting in so many ways. It's just not the right
environment for someone like me. Being on this boat doesn't suit my
loves."

I reached for the water container to fill the kettle. "Bad career
choice, then, eh?"

He pulled a silly face and adopted a mock sales accent: "Come to
the tropics, they said. Get some sunshine!"

Outside it was cold and dreary, the first unsettled weather we'd had
in a week.

Steve scratched the back of his head and yawned. "Well, at least the
wind is going in the right direction for a change. Each miserable little
wave is pushing us one step closer to getting off this fucking thing."

"What would you rather be doing this Sunday morning?" I asked,
placing the kettle on the stove and clicking the lighter.

His face brightened at the thought. "Let me see ... my perfect Sunday morning would be getting up and going for a walk on the beach in

Salcombe, while it's nice and fresh. Then going to Captain Morgan's breakfast house, and having a big bacon and egg sandwich with—" He was interrupted by a low thud, followed by a bucketful of water injecting itself through the sliding hatch and over his head.

"Are you sure?" I chuckled, watching the rivulets trickle down his neck and into his sleeping bag.

Determined not to be done out of his perfect Sunday, Steve soldiered on. "With big thick rashers and a steaming pot of sweet tea. I'd sit and read the Sunday papers until about eleven. Then take my goddaughter and nephew to the beach to build sand castles, or go sailing and find a little cove somewhere and take a picnic. Stop by the Ferry Inn on the way back for a couple of pints."

"And then?"

"Back home, crash out on the sofa and watch a black-and-white war movie until …"

He talked on, building a fantasyland of hearty food and cosy company, a rollicking scene of comfort and good cheer. The kettle came to a squealing boil. I killed the flame and poured hot water into our thermos mugs. The reserve watermaker was still holding out, thank goodness, and despite making an unpleasant grinding sound, so was the last pedal unit.

I popped a teabag into each mug, added milk powder, sugar, and then stirred, thinking of what Steve had said: *Being on this boat doesn't suit my loves.* Outside, the wind howled. A waterlogged sock migrated back and forth in the bilges. It was day forty-one of the voyage.

WITH LESS THAN two hundred miles to go, Steve and I had our second and only other disagreement. Afraid we could miss Hawaii altogether should the wind back to the north and drive us south, Steve favoured a heading of 240 degrees, maintaining our northerly trajectory for as long as possible. I pushed for 210, putting us on the same latitude as Hilo, lessening the chances of being sucked into the notoriously rough Alenuihaha Channel between the Big Island and Maui. There were pros and cons to both arguments, but instead of resorting to yelling at each other like on the Atlantic, Steve and I did something that at one time would have been unthinkable. We settled at 225 degrees, a compromise emblematic of the voyage itself.

On the morning of day fifty-three, the eastern seaboard of the Big Island took shape through a mantle of grey cloud, brought to life like a photographic print in a darkroom developing tray. First into focus were the black lava obelisks of Leleiwi Point, marking the easternmost extent of Hilo Bay. Next came the fuzzy outline of dense tropical greens in the middle distance, verdant slopes merging to drizzling mist. Finally, the mist lifted completely, and the top third of the picture became clear: Mauna Kea's majestic nut-brown slopes towering skyward, its snowy cap glinting in the morning sunlight.

Only now, certain that I wasn't imagining it, I cupped my hands and yelled: "Land ahoy!"

The grinding sound of the pedal unit stopped immediately. Steve joined me in the hatchway, his face stretched with cautious optimism. "Finally," he breathed, eagerly taking in the jagged contours and exquisite colours. "I can't believe we got this close before seeing it."

The previous afternoon, we'd guessed that land was near when the aquamarine water turned to opaque green and scraps of vegetation drifted past. Our flotilla of dorado fish, the same loyal companions that had escorted us all the way from California, sensed it, too, turning back into deeper, cleaner water. By daybreak, the GPS had us a mere ten miles from land, yet there was still no sign of it through the haze. Was the GPS calibrated wrong? Would rocks come crunching through the hull at any moment? We took turns keeping watch on the foredeck, straining into the gloom, listening for the first sound of waves crashing on the alien shore.

With landfall imminent, I rooted in the Rathole for my passport. Unearthing the contents of my canvas wallet was like an exercise in archaeology, rediscovering a cache of artefacts belonging to a bygone age: bank cards, driving licence, keys, passport, library card, address book, and forty-three dollars in US currency. None of these items served any useful purpose at sea, but they were essential instruments for navigating the volatile waters of human civilization. I felt my gut squeeze with the same hollow anxiety that preceded our arrival in Miami. We were about to be catapulted into another dimension, the peace and simplicity of ocean life shattered with the return to meat-grinder expedition logistics.

A white motorboat, *Force Play*, rounded the harbour breakwater. As it drew closer, bouncing through the swell, a set of bronzed legs attached to a grass hula skirt caught my eye. White blossoms bunched around her head and neck, the island beauty leaned over the forward rail, waved, and blew kisses. Standing beside her was an older man, his arm draped casually around her shoulders.

"Blimey," Steve gulped, peering through one of the salt-flecked windows. "I wonder who that dirty lucky bastard is?"

I looked closer. The hat looked familiar.

"Umm. It's your dad, Steve."

It was classic Stuart to rustle up a dusky Hawaiian maiden in the middle of nowhere, the kind of legendary mischief he was famous for, like the strip-o-gram nurse he'd managed to smuggle into Parkview Medical Center following my accident.

Steve blinked. "Hang on, that's not a Hawaiian bird. That's Nancy Sanford!"

Sure enough, the familiar features of our Florida-based coordinator became unmistakable. Another face appeared, one I recognized as

Jake, a producer from the San Francisco-based media company, Video Free America. He was filling in for Kenny, away in some war-torn hellhole. Poor Jake looked white as a sheet. Waving briefly, he set his camera down and began retching over the side.

Another hour of pedalling and *Moksha* bumped alongside the public jetty. I threw a line, a crowd clapped, and real Hawaiian maidens stepped forward this time, looping sweet-smelling leis around our necks in a traditional island welcome.

"Aloha!"

Those first steps on land were unsteady, but nothing compared to the drunken lurches boarding the USCS Charles L. Brown on Christmas Day mid-Atlantic, or arriving in Miami six weeks later. No old dears moaning about their sick cats, either. I found myself facing two boys, their expressions galvanized by an avalanche of impending questions.

"So what's it like pedalling?" asked one, a freckle-faced nine year old with red hair.

"What's your name?" I said.

"Zachary."

"Is this your brother, Zachary?"

"Yes. His name's Jacob."

"Would you and Jacob like to find out?"

The pair looked at each other, their eyebrows raised. Jacob was the older of the two, with dark hair and an old soul behind the heavy-lidded eyes. "You mean right now?" he asked.

I laughed. "No, Steve and I need a little breather and to wash off some of this salt. How about tomorrow? We could go for a spin around the harbour after breakfast."

Zachary pointed to a jolly-faced woman in dark glasses talking to Stuart. "That's our mom. We better ask her first."

While the brothers hurried off to ask permission, I looked around for Steve. He was standing alone at the end of the pier, blue bandana covering his cropped scalp, mind clearly far away—Salcombe, perhaps? And in that moment, I remembered a story he'd once told me, of a fortune teller who came to his childhood home to sell lace to his mother. "You'll be a great traveller," the old gypsy woman told the boy, examining his palms on the doorstep, "but a fool to yourself."

A missing jigsaw piece fell into place: *This is his journey's end,* I thought to myself.

"I'm not going to be pedalling in the expedition anymore," Steve confirmed later that evening. We were having a beer together in the bar of the Naniloa Hotel, where Stuart had arranged a complimentary room for the night. Apart from the seven years that had passed, we could have been back in Paris, drinking Kronenbourg 1664 at two in the morning, discussing his hare-brained idea to circumnavigate the world without motors or the wind. "It's difficult to …" He hesitated.

"You don't need to explain," I said quickly, filling the awkward silence.

He looked at me quizzically.

"That morning on the Bouncy Castle," I continued, "when you described your perfect Sunday. I had an inkling then."

The apprehension fell from his face. "Do you remember the conversation we had in that pub in Dorset all those years ago, Jase?"

I nodded. "We both agreed that if the journey became anything less than wholehearted, we'd quit."

The pledge had become part of our mission statement: *To live fully and enjoy the experience.*

"Well, I think I've worked something out," said Steve. "There's nothing I can pleasurably do with my life on the expedition that I couldn't do better somewhere else. I could justify another few months at sea, wanting to be back on land. But I can't justify another ten years wanting in my heart to be doing something else."

Everyone and his dog would have something to say about this, the British tabloid press in particular, and other gloaters who'd never even met him. *He gave up! Couldn't stand it! Let his partner down!*

It didn't matter. These were the kind of narrow-minded nitwits who would never understand how travel is one of life's greatest paradoxes. Because, as the American author Ursula K. Le Guin once pointed out, "It is good to have an end to journey towards, but it is the journey that matters in the end." And if you're honest and openhearted and strong-minded enough, the journey can evolve to be something else, a stepping stone to wherever you need to go next, learning whatever it is you need to learn: above all, to stay true to yourself, growing to be a healthier and happier person in the process, becoming an asset not a liability to the Earth and its people.

Between Steve and me, nothing more needed to be said. My old friend had solved the gypsy's riddle. By leaving the expedition, he was shunning travel for travel's sake and the danger of becoming a fool to himself. He was following his heart, not his head, and certainly not the expectations of others. He was doing what we both knew to be the right thing to do.

We raised our glasses to the expedition.

THE BIG ISLAND
IRON EDIE

It is the experiences, the memories, the great triumphant joy of living to the fullest extent in which real meaning is found.

—From the journals of CHRISTOPHER JOHNSON MCCANDLESS

S LAP BANG IN THE middle of the Pacific, rising a mere ten feet above sea level, a narrow slip of sand, Tarawa, forms one of thirty-three coral island atolls making up the little-known oceanic kingdom of Kiribati. Formerly a British colony known as the Gilbert and Ellice Islands, this fragile nub of land offered the next resupply point on *Moksha's* long-haul passage to Australia.

I longed to return to the liquid void, be seduced again by the cruel yet passionate embrace of the sea. Empty. Vital. Desolate. Absolute. The mother of all wildernesses beckoned me with her siren call. There would be no distractions on this voyage. Not another human soul. I yearned to strive for and regain the *Samadhi* I'd experienced on the Atlantic and since lost, a state of non-dualistic awareness against which regular, monochrome reality pales in comparison. And this time I would sustain it indefinitely, I told myself.

Of course, if I hadn't been so blinded by hubris back then, I would have known that approaching truth in such a clumsy, cack-handed way is asking for trouble. It's not just a set of fancy clothes you can slip in and out of whenever you feel like it. As with any insight into what Hindu sages referred to as the Supreme Reality, you have to approach truth in a roundabout, almost disinterested way and find it accidentally on purpose. *Not this, not that*, the mystics said. Look straight at it, and you'll see nothing. Peek out of the corner of your mind's eye, however, and maybe, just maybe, if the dots connect and the metaphors align, your perception jogs and truth jumps into focus. But you have to let go immediately to hold onto it.

A paradox.

Before that I needed to walk across the Big Island, ninety miles to Kailua-Kona. From there it was a straight shot to Tarawa, 2,400 miles farther to the west. Steve stayed on to hike with me, and, in his loyal fashion, help prepare *Moksha* for the upcoming voyage. The three-day trek was also an opportunity to invite some expedition friends along.

Edie Leitner was a twenty-six-year-old Spanish teacher from Monterey High School in California, accompanying one of her senior students, Travis Perkins, who'd filmed for the Video Exchange Program. A Waikoloa native, Avery, offered to be our guide. Completing the troop was Scott, *Moksha's* propeller maker, who said he fancied, "a bit of a walk to shake a few pounds."

It was trial by fire. Shouldering sixty-pound packs, we trudged out of Hilo at first light, staggering up the steep incline between the two volcanoes, Mauna Loa and Mauna Kea. By noon we had our first casualty. Claiming he'd gone on holiday by mistake, Scott sat down in the road and refused to move.

"You guys keep going," he said wearily, leaning against a fantastically unwieldy green backpack he'd christened The Green Manalishi after a Fleetwood Mac song. "Me and the old Manalishi are gonna head back."

Only through bribing him with redistribution of the Manalishi's contents would Scott agree to continue. And from that point on, the 250-pound machinist became an engine of determination. By the time the road emerged out of the piddling mist and levelled out at 6,500 feet, he and Travis, who'd earlier complained of knee pain, were unstoppable. Extra weight was added to their packs just to slow the buggers down.

Our route took us past clusters of bobbing hibiscus and 'i'iwi birds dancing in the crimson blossoms of ohia trees. A knowledgeable botanist and ornithologist, Avery struck off on impromptu detours, taking in native curiosities like kipukas, unique island ecosystems marooned by lava. Footsore and grumbling, the group followed.

Leaving Saddle Road and striking off into the Pohakuloa military training area, we picked our way through cowpat-shaped pahoehoe lava fields, taking care not to topple into the mouths of collapsed lava tubes that once served as refuges in times of tribal warfare. Each evening we marched until dark, cooked a hasty meal, then pulled out our sleeping bags and slept like the dead.

On the morning of the fourth day, tired and running low on water, we chanced upon a hunter's cabin with a rainwater collection tank. From here, we picked up the historic Judd Trail leading down to the ocean. Scott's spirits buoyed, breathing new life into his already popular gorilla impressions. A near-constant banter accompanied our descent through soaring stands of eucalyptus, the slapstick babble distracting us from complaining feet and protesting muscles. Edie suffered the worst—her feet by now were a mass of ruptured blisters from ill-fitting boots. Nonetheless, she soldiered on, refusing to slow the pace or be relieved of any of her gear, earning the deserved title "Iron Edie."

"It cannot be bargained with," quoted Scott from *The Terminator* movie. "It cannot be reasoned with. It doesn't feel pity or remorse or fear. And it absolutely will not stop!"

We strode into Kona as one, exhausted, jubilant, and contemplative from our foray into the Hawaiian wilds. "Once I walked across the island of Hawaii in search of happiness," Travis blogged on his return. "And now I no longer know if I am at vacation's end, frantically searching for an epiphany, or still meditating in the lava fields, realizing how terrible if it were true. In the forest, I moved so fast and quietly from one idea to another. Now, life moves so fast I cannot catch up, and it only seems to push me backwards."

MOKSHA WAS HAULED to Kona on a borrowed trailer and parked alongside an open-air Samoan *fale* belonging to an orchid farmer, Lima Tamasese, on the edge of town.* The rest of us—Steve, Nancy, Stuart,

---

* *Fale* is the Samoan word for house. Traditional *fales* are constructed out of local materials such as timber, thatch, coconut fibres, lava, and coral.

his friend Renee from Arizona, and I—got to work scraping barnacles, now withered and putrid, and yanking out the bags of recycling.

Wrap-up from the voyage also included evaluating the Ecological Footprints curriculum. Pupils had written reports to demonstrate their grasp of the coursework, culminating in a list of practical ways to lighten their future footprint and inspire friends and families to do the same. Mary Farmers School in Benicia built worm bins to compost biodegradable waste from the school kitchen, producing soil to grow vegetables. The Nueva School in Burlingame devised their own curriculum extension of students building prototype vehicles for low-impact adventures, such as eleven-year-old Aliya Chaye Weiss's pedal-powered Vacuum Vehicle for a Cleaner Environment.

The *fale* was an effective halfway house between wilderness and civilization, a decompression chamber for Steve and me to unscrew our sea heads and reconnect our land heads. However, without electricity or a phone, the rudimentary shelter lacked somewhat as a base camp from which to launch the next leg. After a fortnight, we moved to the basement-cum-garage of the Thrasher Family, whose two sons, Zak and Jacob, had pedalled *Moksha* around Hilo harbour. A storeroom doubled as a makeshift office, and the garage had enough space to spread out tools and equipment, assemble provisions, and sleep. A tarp slung from the eaves outside protected *Moksha* from the elements.

The only thing was the noise from the acting disciplinarian, Laurie Ann, a larger-than-life pirate queen with the lungs to match.

"Goddammit, Zachary, I told you to make your bed and swab that floor an hour ago!"

The thundering tirades that seeped through the floorboards were unsettling at first ("Them's that dies are the lucky ones!"), until we realized they were just the matriarch's playful way of keeping her mischievous boys in check. For beneath her powerful *mana*, Laurie Ann had the softest heart. The expedition became part of the extended family right from the get-go.

With time to kill before the end of the hurricane season, our efforts returned to education. Local high school students were recruited for the Video and Photo Exchange Programs, and middle schoolers enlisted in papermaking workshops, producing pen pal letters for me to deliver in *Moksha* to schools on Tarawa. A new initiative called Young Explorers saw groups of kids from Kona, some of whom had never travelled beyond the city limits, supervised on daylong mini-expeditions to outlying areas. In all, 1,500 youngsters from twelve schools took part in the various activities. The Kona Public Library hosted a photographic exhibition entitled Step Into My World, displaying black-and-white prints taken by children in North and Central America using the point-and-shoot cameras.

Such devotion of time and energy to educational outreach would have been impossible on previous hiatuses, busy as we were scrabbling around to raise funds. However, the winds of financial fortune had recently veered in our favour. While Steve and I were pedalling from San Francisco, a Colorado court had awarded compensation for pain, suffering, and future complications with my broken legs. The balance after repaying old debts wasn't enough to complete the circumnavigation, but the interest from investing in high-yield technology stocks would cover basic living expenses and the ongoing educational effort.

After years of limping along on $20 donations, the expedition could finally support itself.

HAWAII TO TARAWA
COOKED IN THE COUNTERCURRENT

The mind is its own place, and in itself, can make a heaven of hell, and a hell of heaven.

—JOHN MILTON

May 4, 1999

I'D SEEN KENNY IN some tight spots over the years, doing whatever it took to get The Shot: clinging to the top of a crane as *Moksha* flipped over in the River Exe, leaning out the back of a speeding van as Steve and I puffed up the Pyrenees, or dangling from a light airplane above the Bahamas. This time, though, he was taking things a little too far, floating around the North Pacific with only an air mattress tied around his chest with string for buoyancy.

"Don't drop the bloody thing," I yelled from *Moksha's* hatch, a reference to the digital camcorder he was holding above his head. "We'll never be able to afford another one."

The filmmaker was treading water, sweeping his free hand back and forth to maintain balance. "Stop fussin', ye big gussie. Now do a big loop an' come straight at me. Don't worry, I'll get oot ye way at th' last minute."

The replacement pedal unit felt wonderfully smooth compared to the surviving one we'd limped into Hilo with. As *Moksha* picked up speed, I threw the rudder hard to starboard and watched Mauna Kea glide south through the cockpit windows. The boat came full circle, and I straightened up and made a beeline for the Scotsman's bobbing head.

Earlier, punch drunk with exhaustion, I'd struck out from Kona harbour in brilliant sunshine with a bundle of green tea leaves lashed to *Moksha's* bow in keeping with Polynesian seafaring tradition. We'd slept little the previous night, thanks in part to Laurie Ann regaling us with sea shanties as she bagged the last of the dehydrated veggies in the garage. Egged on by Jose Cuervo tequila, a case of Steinlager talls, and Aunty Ta-Ta, who had a penchant for flashing her breasts, our Hawaiian host had rounded off her exemplary hospitality by singing "All For Me Grog" and other salty favourites until the wee hours.

"Ookay."

Twisting my head, I was relieved to see Kenny plus camera still afloat through the stern window. Steering blind the last fifty feet, I'd half expected to feel the jarring thud of wood on bone.

"Hang oan a minute, I think ma Thermarest is leakin'!"

I stopped pedalling and stuck my head out of the hatch. The cameraman was already well astern, looking small and vulnerable surrounded by so much water. Noticeably lower in the water, too.

"Ahm definitely sinkin'. Come 'n get me, willya?"

I watched him drift further. "That depends," I replied.

"Whaddya mean *depends*. Oan what?"

"The twenty bucks you owe me."

Kenny scowled. "What twen'y bucks?"

"The twenty bucks I lent you in the boozer the other night, remember?"

"The fuck you did. Stop pissin' aboot, Jas'n."

"I was thinking of adding a little interest. Say, twenty per cent?"

Like all Scots, Kenny was chary when it came to money. Earlier, after transferring from the support boat, he'd told me the Scottish cure for seasickness was to hang over the side with a fifty pence piece between one's teeth.

I froze, pointing to a swirl in the water. "Oh, shit."

"Wha' is it?"

"Shark."

The colour drained from his face. "Really?"

"Nah. Just kidding."

"Bastard," he spluttered. "Noo come an' get me, ye fucker, before I droon along wi' ye shitein' video camera!"

Quarter of a mile off our port beam, the snowy canvas of *Goodewind* luffed in the light breeze. Built for speed, the fifty-two-foot cutter looked awkward and ungainly idling along at three knots. I retrieved Kenny and manoeuvred alongside for him to catch his ride back to Kona. The sun was setting as we made the switch. Then the dreadful goodbyes began.

Leaning between the two hulls, Steve and I grasped each other's forearms like we had leaving Greenwich all those years ago. My friend looked dishevelled in his hessian sunhat, unshaven and watery-eyed from fatigue in the build up to departure. Or was there something else?

"Are you sure you're okay with this?" I asked, feeling a lump form in my throat. "Taking *Moksha,* I mean."

He gazed down at his creation. "Yes, yes." He smiled. "At the end of the day, she's just a boat. But you take good care of yourself. Always keep the safety line clipped to your ankle, okay?"

Good old Steve, I thought, *fussing till the last.* "Thanks, mate. Thanks for everything." I shoved hard against the larger vessel.

Stuart appeared beside his son. "The same angel in Portugal promised me you'd be alright, Jase."

I smiled and waved. "That's good to know. Thanks, Stuey."

Given her head at last, *Goodewind* surged forward and her wings swelled majestically like a swan in flight, demonstrating how much quicker and easier it would be to sail to Tarawa instead of pedal. The skipper, Captain Nancy, gathered speed and spun the wheel, setting a course back to Kona. I kept waving and waving, changing arms, and waving some more. *Goodewind* shrank to a fleck of white in a universe of blue, and then she was gone.

Suddenly, I was alone, the only living thing as far as the eye could see.

"Start of a new chapter on the expedition." My voice faltered as I panned the camcorder westward, courage stalled in the face of such overwhelming vastness and the scale of the task at hand. "Ahead, two thousand four hundred miles away, is Tarawa, my next port of call. It'll be like trying to find a needle in a haystack, but I have to find it."

Putting the camera down, I just stood there, absorbing the boat's corkscrew motion with my knees and soaking in the ambience of this new world—a familiar world, yet strangely different now that I was the only one in it. *This is what you wanted,* I reminded myself, *weeks of meditative contemplation, all alone.* It would take around a month to make the transition, I estimated, for the clutter of civilization to fall away and the emptiness of wilderness to take hold, paving the way for *Samadhi.*

My ailing spirits rose at the prospect.

One prospect that didn't fill me with enthusiasm, however, was crossing the Inter Tropical Convergence Zone (ITCZ), the 400-mile-wide countercurrent between two and eight degrees north of the equator. The bane of mariners since the Age of Sail, the doldrums were defined by frequent thunderstorms, little or no wind, and a flat, torpid ocean endured for weeks on end by the becalmed sailor. Water spilling in from the Northern Hemisphere met water pouring in from the south, the two bodies of water converging and funnelling east towards Mexico. To reach the Southern Hemisphere and ultimately Australia, I needed to punch through roughly two hundred miles of contrary current, something the sailing buffs in San Francisco had predicted almost impossible in a human-powered craft.

Darkness fell as I contemplated all of this and my first night at sea alone. Sleeping without a pair of eyeballs trained on the horizon was one of my secret fears. Yes, I had the all-round white light and the Ocean Sentry radar detector to warn of approaching ships, but it was a well-known fact that commercial vessels often switched off their radar once free of the busy coast. *Moksha* was effectively a sitting duck while I slumbered, a chunk of glorified driftwood waiting to get nailed.

Reaching inside the Rathole, I retrieved my ocean ring from a rusty hook above the electrical panel, slipped it on my ring finger, and reaffirmed my vow to the sea: *From now on, we are one.* I switched on the red compass light, shuffled into the pedal seat, and got to work. Then something curious happened. The air around the hatch filled with the sound of beating wings. A solitary seabird, brown with white markings and a long conical beak, landed with a gentle thud on the stern deck.

So I wasn't alone after all. *Stuart's guardian angel?* I thought whimsically, glad of the company.

IF IT WAS, the angel appeared to be suffering from some intestinal disorder. I awoke next morning to a large pile of dung on the stern solar panel. The culprit—a juvenile Red-footed Booby, according to my bird book—was long gone. That one of God's messengers might have needed a lavatory as much as I did the company had never occurred to me.

From then on, I had running battles with these shitehawks, renowned cadgers of the ocean highways, to keep *Moksha* from being plastered in guano. As if I didn't have anything better to do. By the time I pedalled, cooked, ate, navigated, wrote an update for the website, replied to email, set assignments for classrooms enrolled in the ongoing Ecological Footprints curriculum, and shooed away the boobies, barely a minute remained.

At least getting enough sleep was no longer an issue with the Rathole all to myself. Still, after only a week, I began lapsing into bouts of lassitude. It was harder to keep motivated, I found, without another human being to lend a competitive edge, a witness to any slacking. To stay productive, I divided my living space into four areas—office, kitchen, bedroom, and recreation—and formalized my routine like a work-at-home freelancer. No less than fourteen hours a day were dedicated to the office, divided into two-hour pedal shifts. I took meal breaks on the passenger seat, allowing ten minutes for mid-morning tea, half an hour for breakfast and lunch, and a full hour to cook and eat dinner. Sleep in the Rathole was limited to six hours in every twenty-four. For recreation, the fore and aft decks were important spaces to occupy for a minimum of five minutes each day. Watching the sun go down with a mug of tea was still the nearest thing to getting out of the house and going for a walk. I even did a little yoga out there, such as the space allowed.

Then there was the ocean itself. As *Moksha* slipped towards the equator and daytime temperatures climbed, diving in after a sweltering shift became my most prized psychological carrot. The pencil dots on the chart boasted fifty-mile-plus days now that I was clear of the unpredictable winds and currents around Hawaii and back in the Northeast Trades. Even so, in order to hit Tarawa, I needed to make one mile south for every two west. After a fortnight this meant altering course to due south, 180 degrees, resulting in water slopping over the side and everything remaining drenched inside the central cabin. A week of this and my nerves began to fray, and my arse turned baboon-like from the constant chaffing. I awoke after one particularly tumultuous night to find three flying fish using the cockpit as an aquarium, and a further twenty-six lying dead out on deck. When I sat down to start my first pedal shift, something cold and slippery sprang to life, another scaly stowaway, launching me six inches into the air.

Lucky for him, I was vegetarian.

On the twenty-first day of the voyage, an American warship appeared on the horizon. I switched on the VHF and requested a radio check. It was just an excuse for a chat, of course. I hadn't spoken to another soul in three weeks. After three attempts, a laconic voice responded: *"Muckshower,* this is *USS Boxer."*

"USS Boxer, this is *Moksha.* Radio check, please. Over."

"Muckshower, you're loud and clear."

"Also, could you tell me if my boat is showing up on radar? I'm about three miles off your port beam."

"That's a negative."

"It's only a small boat. Pedal powered. No motor or sails. So it'll be moving pretty slowly."

"That's a negative."

And that, I concluded from the clipped, disinterested tone was that. I turned my attention instead to a flying fish being pursued by a dorado under the water and a bird above. The plucky little fish leapt and plunged, predators hot on its flicking tail. The radio then sprang back to life.

"Err, *Muckshower*, this is *USS Boxer.*"

I absentmindedly unclipped the microphone and told the radio operator to go ahead, riveted as I was to the fate of the flying fish. But there was nowhere for the hapless creature to go. In a dazzling display of aerial acrobatics, the bird snatched the fish from the jaws of the snapping dorado and swallowed it whole.

"Muckshower, you ain't that crazy sonofabitch going around the world are you? The one we read about in the *West Hawaii Today* a few weeks ago."

I replied that yes, I was indeed that crazy sonofabitch. And like many opening conversations I'd had with Americans, it wasn't long before we were on to the Queen Mum, tepid beer, sponge cakes, and cricket. The unbridled Anglophilia was further fuelled by the revelation that the *Boxer* was named after a British warship captured during the War of 1812.

Ten minutes later, the operator said he had to clear the frequency. "But before we let you go, *Muckshower,* the first officer wanted to know if you'd like a salad for lunch."

I laughed. "Don't tease me."

"You said you were out of fruit," the operator went on. "We'd be happy to send over a chopper."

I'd eaten the last of my oranges two days before, a religious experience made even more so by the idea of no fresh fruit or greens passing my lips for another two months.

"That's very kind," I replied. "The only thing is I'm not a big salad fan."

The truth was I could have eaten a dozen salads with the calories I was burning, and an offer from the world's most powerful armed service to airlift some sliced tomato on a bed of lettuce was almost too priceless to pass up. But scrambling a helicopter would have taken several hundred litres of aviation fuel. And what kind of message did that send to classrooms looking at ways to reduce fossil fuel emissions?

AFTER A MONTH at sea, the dreaded saltwater sores appeared, as they had on the Atlantic. The result of sweat pores clogged with salt, they started out as minor skin swellings before developing into full-blown septic boils spewing a stream of disgusting, foul-smelling pus. They were unhygienic, painful, and impossible to get rid of, especially those exposed to the most friction like the ones on my buttocks.

This was also the point on the Atlantic that I'd undergone a cognitive shift. Those first forty days and forty nights amounted to a self-imposed period of withdrawal, of clawing desperately at the threads of a past life, rummaging junkie-like through crumbling boxes of freeze-frame images, sepia movie clips, and sound bites snatched from the muffled recesses of memory—childhood, family, school, relationships, hopes and fears, triumphs and regrets. Pedalling at night was especially conducive for this wool-gathering, a form of posthumous inventorying by a ghost haunting the attic of an old house, free to listen to and visualize the people living and laughing in the rooms below, but powerless to reconnect.

Then had come the shedding of the old skin, releasing the mind-set required to function on land and transitioning to one more suited to Planet *Moksha.* My attention, brought to heel through meditation, had narrowed around the present, magnifying awareness like a microscope. The transformation happened quickly enough to take the form of a resurrection: death to the old life, rebirth to the new. The hauntings faded. So, too, the memories. Drained of colour and vitality, they became redundant, shrivelling to dry, bloodless artefacts pinned like dusty moths to the gossamer-thin tapestry of time, making way for the clarity of mind preceding *Samadhi.*

On this voyage, however, things were turning out rather different. Alone and slave to the constant demands of technology, I'd found little time to meditate. My awareness remained scattered, pulled every which way. I was also finding it very lonely. Rather than nurturing One Pointed Attention, I sought out companionship instead.

"Come on, you greedy little bugger."

After each meal I would clean my plate over the side, drawing a darting posse of black-and-white-striped pilot fish from under *Moksha's* belly. The plumpest one I'd nicknamed Homer, as in Simpson. He'd become something of a pet.

"There you go, Homes. Get any fatter and you'll be feeding the five thousand."

On day thirty-two, I donned flippers and a mask and went over the side to scrub barnacles. The crustaceans were already two inches long and growing in a thick forest, slowing *Moksha's* speed considerably. I worked methodically down each side, scraping with a plastic food lid, fussed all the while by the territorial pilot fish. Reaching the stern, I noticed that a family of biscuit-coloured crabs had taken up residence around the rudder. The idea of *Moksha* supporting a web of symbiotic relationships rather appealed to me. The crabs got sanctuary. The barnacles filtered microscopic particles of food using their feathery legs. The pilot fish gobbled my leftovers. And I got—what? A sense of community, I suppose. Companionship. I decided to leave the rudder barnacles alone.

Next day, the saltwater sores got much worse.

THE SOUND OF scratching woke me. This wasn't unusual. The sea anchor rope coiled around the hatch often chafed in a northeasterly. But this was different. Sharper. More insistent. Like gnawing against the hull. Moving slowly from the bow to the stern.

Then nothing.

In that semi-lucid state between sleep and full consciousness, I lay staring at the roof of the Rathole, listening. Had I imagined it? After a minute or so, I reached for the handrail, took the weight off my upper body, and heaved my head and shoulders out into the cockpit. The sky was deep azure and the wind blowing fifteen knots. *Perfect pedalling day,* I thought. *Might even set the highest mileage of the voyage—sixty miles.*

I was about to slide the rest of the way out when *Moksha* suddenly tipped to starboard, slamming me against the bulkhead.

The scratching was back, sounding like a rasp against the gunwale.

THUNK!

Something dense and rubbery landed on the stern deck. Turning my head, I saw a long, trunk-like arm studded with grey suction cups coiling up the wind generator pole. My heart skipped a beat. I knew what this was.

THUNK!

Another tentacle dropped into the central compartment. It began groping, working the cockpit for food. I yanked myself back into the Rathole and slammed the hatch just in time. The tentacle lunged, sending volleys of suckers like fistfuls of wet clay against the tinted Perspex.

Roused by the hunt, yet more arms were snaking out of the water. Then something truly awful: red, swollen, pulsating, grotesque, a dripping abdomen hauled itself aboard. *Moksha* tilted farther to starboard and water poured into the cockpit. Even with both bulkheads secured, the boat couldn't possibly support the weight of the creature.

I had two choices. Either drown in the sleeping compartment, or take my chances outside.

Fumbling for the dive knife, I opened the hatch and pushed into the flooded cabin. Leathery arms embraced me instantly, their tiny barbs hooking into my skin. I struggled, but it was hopeless. A dull, liquid eye as big as a hubcap watched impassively as the tentacles drew me closer. Two seabirds swooped silently overhead. The ocean, blue and indifferent, rolled away into nothing.

Click! Click! Click!

The air filled with a putrid stench. A fold of skin on the monster's body pulled back to reveal an ebony skull working back and forth like mechanical shears.

Click! Click! Click!

I raised my arm to plunge the knife, but I was paralyzed, my hand stayed by some invisible force. Something was scratching at my stomach now—the beak straining for its meal. Shards of molten pain ripped through my torso, and I opened my mouth to scream.

IT WAS THE screaming that woke me. I sat bolt upright, drenched in sweat, heart pounding like a drum.

It's just a dream, a bad dream.

The same bad dream I'd had five nights in a row, and always ending the same: being disembowelled by the Kraken.

Gingerly, I levered myself out of the Rathole. My body had become a mass of raised welts and oozing sores, a second layer of boils erupting over the first. The most severe, ulcerated and bleeding, were flaring up around the fracture sites on my lower legs.

A freshwater shower was the obvious solution—but impossible, of course. Determined to find an alternative cure, I'd been experimenting with four affected areas. I dabbed my left buttock three times a day with calamine lotion, the right with a little drinking water. For my arms I got more creative: a squirt of WD40 under the right, and a recipe involving stewed cabbage emailed by a fifth-grade class in Indiana under the left (I was desperate enough to try anything by this point). The fracture sites I left as a control.

Within a day, the WD40 showed signs of drying the abscesses but did nothing to alleviate the headaches, bouts of nausea, and numbness in the fingers of my right hand. Guessing dehydration to be the cause, I'd started taking electrolytes to restore essential body salts. Or was it some nutritional deficiency?

Sitting delicately on the passenger seat, flinching at each movement of the boat, I contemplated my diet. The largely unappetizing rations of the last two voyages had inspired custom preparation for this one: carrots, broccoli, mushrooms, squash, and peppers desiccated in multistorey dryers in Laurie Ann's garage. Hardier vegetables like onions, cabbage, ginger, and garlic lasted well as they were. Porridge and rice were still staples. Protein came from dried bean curd and tofu sealed in aseptic boxes. Perhaps I was missing an essential vitamin or mineral?

Unable to face anything sweet, I made some black, sugarless tea and started my first shift. Pedalling offered the only respite from the sores. As soon as the cranks stopped turning, they shrieked for attention.

On my lunch break I fired up the satellite terminal and downloaded email. An anxious message from April warned that my blog entries were starting to sound like gibberish. Acting on a hunch that dehydration wasn't the root cause, she'd taken the liberty of contacting a dermatologist fished from the Yellow Pages. Doctor Sharon Kessler urged that I call her immediately, despite it being late on a Sunday evening in Colorado.

"This is so clear," the voice said cheerfully. "Like you're just down the road at the Loaf 'N Jug gas station. I can hear the water, the grinding of the pedals."

I was pedalling as I listened, the satellite phone connected to an ice hockey puck-sized antenna on the cabin roof.

"So, my first question," continued the doctor, "is what in the world gave you the idea to pedal across the Pacific Ocean?"

What she really meant was: Has society rejected you? Did your mother drop you on your head when you were a baby? Only an insane person would do something like that, my friend, and therein lies your prognosis.

Doctor Kessler spent the next few minutes building a patient history. When I listed my symptoms—numbness in the fingers, nausea, recurrent nightmares, suppurating sores—her voice turned serious.

"My concern is that if you do have something like a Staph infection, and you're getting boils as you're describing, that could secondarily infect the titanium rods in your legs. Then you'd have an osteomyelitis, which would require IV antibiotics and removal of the rods. How far from a hospital are you, by the way?"

"Right now, about a thousand miles."

"Oh, God. And how long would it take you to get to land if you had to?"

I thought for a moment. No coastguard cutter or helicopter could reach me. "If I'm lucky," I replied, "and I get picked up by a ship, then a week to ten days maybe—assuming they're heading in the right direction."

"Ha! Well, shoot. That ain't gonna work."

I called again the next morning, giving the dermatologist time to consult an infectious disease specialist. Meanwhile, my condition had deteriorated: shaking chills and a fever of 104 degrees.

"So what's the verdict, doc?"

"Well, we're pretty certain you've picked up something from the water while swimming." This was news. The ocean around *Moksha* looked pristine. "Seawater is filthy," the doctor explained. "Slime, fish pee, and the same kinds of bacteria you find on land. Also, some marine pathogens that can be really nasty, like one called Vibrio."

"How would it have got into my body, though?"

"Through the open sores. That way the microorganism could enter your bloodstream directly. It wouldn't take long for an infection to become systemic."

It took me a few seconds to process the seriousness of her words. "So, you're saying I have blood poisoning?" It made sense. Nausea, headaches, fever, and fatigue were symptomatic of a number of ailments other than dehydration, including septicaemia.

"That's what we believe," the doctor replied gravely.

"How long do I have?"

"Forty-eight hours. Probably less."

Hearing this, I remembered that my mother's stepfather had been gored by an African buffalo in Kenya and died of sepsis a few days later.

Doctor Kessler interrupted my ruminations. "Do you have any antibiotics with you?"

I pulled the first aid box out from under the pedal seat and thumbed through the orange plastic bottles. "There's some stuff in here that Doctor Danylchuk gave me for my legs, but it's three years out of date."

"Is there a name?"

I squinted at the faded lettering. "Cipro ... floxa ... cin."

A snort rang through the earpiece. "You must have a guardian angel looking over you, Jason. Without a specific blood test, Cipro is one of the few antibiotics that'll kill a wide spectrum of pathogens, including Vibrio."

"But it's expired."

"It doesn't matter. In tablet form they last a lot longer than the expiration."

Sure enough, within 24 hours of taking the first 750-milligramme tablet, my fever, headaches and nausea had subsided. Feeling gradually returned to my fingers, and after three days my appetite was back to normal. Even the sores were drying up without the mysterious healing qualities of WD40.

In the weeks that followed, I found myself musing on the ambiguous nature of technology. The wisdom of integrating it into the expedition was something I'd seriously questioned in the early stages of the voyage. The satellite phone, the laptop, all the other gizmos, they were like time sinks, draining every waking minute, making One Pointed Attention impossible. In the rush to complete all the daily tasks, my awareness had thinned, rolled out like pie dough to a shallower and shallower crust, allowing none of the requisite depth for *Samadhi*. Yet, on this occasion, technology had surpassed itself. Along with the antibiotics and Doctor Kessler's detective skills, it had afforded the greatest liberation of all.

Survival.

I KNEW I was in the doldrums proper when I awoke on the morning of the forty-fifth day to an ocean of glass and deafening silence. Standing there in the hatchway, an actor poised on a liquid stage, I held up a mug of tea to greet the dawn, blood pulsing in my ears and a high-pitched ringing like a badly tuned radio set.

Then the squalls started, furious downpours unleashed by swollen gobs of sooty cloud. For days I'd watched the southern horizon light up with intermittent flashes. The sea felt warmer to the touch, and the air had that saturated, prickly feel to it preceding a storm. Anxious about lightning, I emailed John Oman, webmaster of the adventure site that hosted my blog. His response was far from reassuring. Lightning had been known to strike unprotected boats, he wrote, hurtling down the mast and blowing a hole through the hull.

In *Moksha's* case, the metal wind generator pole would be the conductor. I rifled through the stern compartment for the cable lock to my bicycle (I carried as much overland gear as I could to save on transoceanic shipping) and the steel handle from the electric watermaker. Incorporating a fork and other random bits of hardware, I jury-rigged a lightning conductor between the pole and the water. *Lightning doesn't like going around corners,* John had advised, *so make the route as direct as possible.*

Aided by water sweeping south into the countercurrent, bisecting the first two hundred miles of the ITCZ was easy. But at five degrees north, approximately halfway across, I hit a wall. The Coriolis effect caused by the Earth's rotation drew water up from the Southern Hemisphere and sent it east at one and a half knots. The countercurrent had me boxed in, unable to make headway south or west.

All I could do was keep pedalling. Historic records showed seasonal variations in the width of the countercurrent and occasional eddies that connected separate bodies of water through subsurface currents. Perhaps I'd get lucky? That first day I pedalled for eighteen hours, managing ten miles good before slumping exhausted into the Rathole. Four hours later, I switched on the GPS and discovered to my horror that I was back where I'd started from the previous morning. The second day was the same. So, too, the third. And the fourth...

When *Moksha* was moving forward, there was always hope. Even if the conditions were awful, the inside of the boat was swamped, and the salt sores relentless, as long as I advanced at least a few miles each day, my legs could keep moving. But hope became a very difficult thing to sustain while pedalling on the spot, going nowhere. At first it was contact with the outside world that kept me distracted from the misery of the position fixes on the chart. A friend would call the satellite phone from a remote office in her Silicon Valley technology company, and every day my father would send me one of his "feeble jokes."

Q: Why did the seagull cross the ocean?

A: To get to the other tide.

By the second week in the countercurrent, though, hope of ever escaping its clutches began to fade. They were dark times, becoming darker with each passing day. *Ran out of reading material today*, I scribbled in my journal one morning. *A terrifying prospect. For now I am fully at the mercy of my own mind.*

It was day fifty-six, the day things started to go awry.

A Grey-backed Tern getting hit by the wind generator was the trigger. I circled back to where the bird lay in the water—head down, wings splayed—and snatched the body as *Moksha* drifted past. At first glance it looked okay. *Just stunned*, I thought. Then I noticed a dent in the right side of the bird's skull, pushing the eyeball from its socket.

Terns often came near the boat, hovering and fussing. It was only a matter of time before one was hit. Still, I was furious with myself. The twelve-volt batteries were fully charged, and the turbine had been running unnecessarily. I railed first at my stupidity. Then I railed at the fishes.

"Hey. Brit fecker. Why don't you pick on someone your own size?" I knew that accent from somewhere. Harsh. Northern Irish. Like my old friend from Belfast. "Oi'm Gary wi' the IRA."

I was leaning over the side, scrubbing the porridge pan. "Oh yeah? Well, I'd keep your big Irish nose out of this if I were you, *Gary wi' the IRA.*"

"Or else h'wat?"

"Else I'll kick you off this fucking boat."

He laughed. "You and whose army? Listen pal, if you don't do what oi tell you to do, whaen oi tell you to do it, oi'm gonnae blow your feckin balls off."

We bickered for a while. Then another voice cut in.

"Vat are you doingk?"

Again, the accent was familiar. German. Unmistakably thick. Like the old U-boat commander we'd met on Madeira part way across the Atlantic.

"Heinz?"

"Jawohl."

"What are you doing here?"

"I heff been vatching you making a peegs ear of der voyage, goingk around ent around fer two veeks now. Are you losingk your mind?"

"Well, funny you should mention it."

"Tell me, Englander, heff you ever gone around der harn?"

"The what?"

"Der harn."

"The Horn? No, I haven't."

"Den you are jest a pup. You need a real captain viz real experience of der sea to get you out of zis countercurrent."

The next day we were joined by an obnoxious Frenchman, his mangled Franglais pinched straight from *Monty Python and the Holy Grail.*

"Aagh shatupayaface, Engleesh fool. Your muzer was a hamster, and your fazer smelled of elderberries. I fart in your general direction, Engleesh peeg-dog."

"And you are?"

"Serge. And ah am zer one who should be running sings around 'ere!"

The situation was getting out of hand. "Right," I said firmly. "This is my boat. My rules."

"Go boil your bottom, *Rosbif,*" scoffed Serge.

"Shoite yer are, Brit fecker," seconded Gary.

"Jawohl! Shtick it, Englander pigk."

Clearly, I was entering the arena of the insane. But who cared? As long as in my own mind I felt sane, I could keep pedalling. That was all that mattered.

"I vud fery much like der sauerkraut tonight," Heinz said as I considered dinner options for that evening.

Serge was the first to object. "Eat my kerck, Kraut faggot. Vee 'ave none of zat sheet on zis boat."

"French *schweinhund*. You heff no taste!"

"You sink you are a connoisseur, German? You are a potato wiz the face of a guinea pig and zer brains of a cheese sandwich. Up yours, *putain.*"

"Yer all ayte shoite," interrupted Gary. "A nice pint 'o Guinness, tho'. That'd really hit the spot now, wouldn't it fellas?"

"Ah non, zer Irish obsession wizzat dizgusting bog water."

"Feck ye, Serge. May a thousands hairy dicks ravage your sister on the grave 'o your dead ma."

And so on.

Outside of these comic interludes, my resolve was beginning to crumble. The days were passing. *Moksha* was going nowhere. Despair closed in like a giant wad of chloroform, dulling the senses, petrifying brain cells, deadening the impetus to keep going. A Canadian disk jockey interviewed me via the Iridium satellite phone.

"Ever feel like givin' up?" he asked.

"No," I lied. "Never."

Only that morning, day fifteen in the countercurrent, I'd broken down in the bottom of the boat, pathetic, weeping, wallowing in an orgy of self-pity under the midday sun. *I have nothing more to give,* I whispered to myself. And yet, as I was to be reminded in the coming days and weeks, there is nearly always something more to give. "The body is capable of immense feats of endurance," I'd once written in my Atlantic journal, "but only if the mind buys into it." From creating fictional friends to poking a finger through the rice paper of *nothing more to give,* all it takes is a mental shift. The pliant mechanism of the human imagination can invent whatever the physical body needs to prevail.

The wall was there. I could feel it: the countercurrent, the mind-bending GPS readings, the utter hopelessness and despair. A jog in perspective, however, and things looked quite different. There was no wall. It was all mind. Every last scrap of it.

You keep going because you have to, I told myself.
It was as simple as that. Pedalling on the spot was better than going
backwards. Better than being taken like a leaf on the wind until the
food ran out and I starved.

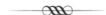

FITTINGLY, GIVEN MY state of mind, it took a vegetable to spring me
from the countercurrent. For weeks *Moksha* had been hovering thirty
nautical miles east of the International Date Line, the imagined de-
marcation between today and tomorrow. For that same period I'd been
saving the last of my onions. Once across the north-south time divide,
which also denoted the meridian farthest from Greenwich, I planned to
celebrate the circumnavigation halfway point by sautéing the onion in
olive oil and livening up an otherwise bland evening meal.

I checked the bulb obsessively like a prize vegetable grower, fantasizing how good it would taste: savoury, full flavoured, and deliciously
crunchy. On the nineteenth day in the doldrums, I noticed a few black
spots on the outer leaves. Terrified that I might lose my beloved vegetable to mould, I abandoned all efforts south and shifted my sights
to the more tangible goal of tomorrow. If fate had conspired to keep
the southern edge of the countercurrent beyond my reach, perhaps
travelling forward in time would help break the cycle and turn my luck
around?

The strategy paid off. A random back eddy allowed me to claw west,
and two days later, on July 3, 1999, at exactly 2156 Greenwich Mean
Time (GMT), *Moksha* crossed the International Date Line escorted by
sixteen dorado, five pilot fish, and eleven crabs the size of a silver dollar.

There was no red ribbon. No banner announcing, "Welcome to Tomorrow!" Just flat, pellucid water as far as the eye could see. The GPS
rounded out to 180:00:00, and I let out a loud whoop. It had taken five

long human-powered years to get this far from Greenwich in East London—half a world away, literally. Then the digits on the screen began counting down: 179:59:59 … 179:59:58 … 179:59:57 … When it was all zeros, I'd be back where I started.

Now in the Eastern Hemisphere, I readopted a southerly course and resigned myself once again to the lot of a caged hamster, spinning its wheel, going nowhere. At the minimum, I was determined to maintain my position. Slipping back into "yesterday" was too depressing a scenario to let happen.

The following afternoon, a riffle of air came skimming across the water from the southeast. I leaned forward in the open hatchway, straining for the cooling effect on my face—no matter how brief. But instead of petering out, the flurry strengthened to a steady breeze, and soon I felt the ocean rouse from its long stasis and stir beneath me. For weeks, any wind had been the by-product of thunderstorms, blowing from all points of the compass before fizzling out altogether. This, on the other hand, was constant and from a uniform direction.

The Southeast Trades, at last!

"So, VEE ESCAPED der countercurrent after awl, *ja?*"

"Yes, Heinz. We got lucky. The southern edge must have come up to meet us, otherwise we'd still be in it."

"Vat do you mean, lucky? It voz my expert seamanship, der golden touch off der old *U-boot* commander."

"Rabbis Kraut *salope*. It was sanks to me, *Le Fleur de Courage*, zat your zorry azzes are not still in zer doldrums!"

"Shoite to the lot o' yer. The IRA is the raisin that we're oyt o' there."

Having kept me company through the worst of it, my crewmates were now more vocal than ever. However, the voyage wasn't in the bag yet.

The next few days passed smoothly enough. *Moksha* resumed her pre-ITCZ performance of fifty-mile days, and a red-footed booby, the same species of dung monger that had left me a steaming pile of manure the first night of the voyage, provided hours of entertainment trying to balance on one of the wind generator shrouds. I even felt fit enough to go over the side and clear barnacles one last time, first sealing the residual salt sores with lithium grease, a suggestion from the students at Budmouth College in Dorset who were following the voyage. I was close to finishing when a giant head loomed in my peripheral vision. Panic-stricken, I yanked myself aboard using the safety lines and accidentally dislodged the claw hammer I kept lashed to my waist for protection. Watching the makeshift weapon plummet into the abyss, I noticed that the killer shark was actually one of the friendly dorados, its head magnified out of all proportion by the thickness of my mask.

The hammer was an important tool for which I had no spare, and I cursed myself for being so jumpy. But the next day, something scraped along the underside of the hull, and then the pedal system locked up. I reached forward to unclip The Dog's Bollocks and caught sight of a long, ventral fin gliding past the starboard windows. It was an oceanic white-tipped shark, *Carcharhinus longimanus*, according to my quick reference guide to pelagics, described by the famed oceanographer Jacques Cousteau as "the most dangerous of all sharks," responsible for more human fatalities than all other shark species combined.

The modest eight-footer slipped nonchalantly away, made a big right-handed loop, and came in for another go.

CLUNK!

Moksha's flashing propeller obviously posed a toothsome meal to the hungry shark, so much so the predator was having difficulty appreciating the hardness of stainless steel. A few seconds later, the cranks released, allowing me to carry on pedalling for the time it took the seed-brained brute to make another loop and repeat the process.

This went on for over an hour.

By July 12, I was seventy miles from Tarawa. The final approach called for every scrap of seamanship and navigational knowledge I'd picked up over the years to negotiate the inter-island currents and enter the west-facing lagoon at exactly one hour before high tide. Too early, and I risked being blown past the atoll while waiting for the tide to change; next stop, the Solomon Islands, eleven hundred miles away. Too late, and I could run aground on the reef like the scores of landing craft wrecked in the amphibious assault of Tarawa by US Marines on November 20, 1943.*

That evening, day seventy-one of the voyage, the handle on the desalinator pump came apart. *Not a complete disaster*, I reassured myself. *There's still the emergency spare in the grab bag.* This was the same little pump that had kept Steve and me alive for thirty-nine days pedalling from San Francisco to Hawaii. Although since being serviced, the pump produced a few mouthfuls of glue-like tasting water, and then refused to make another drop.

Disaster!

There should have been twelve gallons of reserve drinking water in the ballast bags, but in the countercurrent, doing whatever it took to keep from going backwards, I'd reassigned my daily two hours of pumping water to pedalling and consumed the twelve gallons instead. The plan was to replenish once free of the doldrums, but this hadn't happened, of course. What were the chances of both watermakers failing?

Apart from occasional nibbles on a PowerBar, I stopped eating (food

---

* Because of a neap tide, something naval battle planners failed to anticipate, the four-foot-draught Higgins boats were unable to clear the reef, forcing the marines to wade ashore.

only required more water to digest). I rounded up every pot, pan, and Tupperware container I could find and lashed them to the cabin roof. A shower swept through in the early hours of the morning. By sun-up, I had enough rainwater to fill a cup.

If I had to choose between dying of dehydration in a desert or on an ocean, I wrote in my journal, *I'd go for desert. There is something fundamentally perverse in being so thirsty yet surrounded by so much water.*

Shortly after dawn on the morning of day seventy-three, a ribbon of grey marked the western horizon. The sight of land was tremendous. Obscure shapes became well-defined features as the morning wore on: bungalows with colourful roofs, dusty clearings carved by sunlight, and cars speeding along a narrow causeway lined with coconut palms. Tarawa, in all its tropical wonder, beckoned.

I took a break to stand in the hatch and soak it all in.

"Land, looks mighty gran', doesn't it?" said Gary.

"It most certainly does," I agreed. "What's the first thing you'll do when we make landfall, Gary?"

"Find a boozer, a Guinness, some fanny, a room."

"Teepical Irish peeg-dog," spat Serge. "Always sinking of your belly and your kerck. 'Ow about"—the Frenchman's voice turned soft and dreamy—"smelling zer flowers, feeling zer earth in your 'ands, and zer sand between your toes. Listening to birds singing in zer trees."

"For vonce," admitted Heinz, "I heff to agree wiz der Frenchman. I, too, em looking forvard to feelingk der ground under der feet, ent der sound off human lafter, ent musick. Awl dose sings missingk out on der vaater."

Listening to my comrades' banter, I was hit by a disconcerting thought. One of the books I'd been reading while pedalling was *A Pattern of Islands* written by a young administrative officer, Arthur Grimble, posted to the Gilbert and Ellice Islands in 1914. The author's observations were amusing and astute, especially those inevitable first impressions spawned by the collision of two utterly dissimilar cultures. Rolling up in one of the farthest-flung corners of the British Empire, the quintessential English gent found himself hopelessly at sea with the ways and customs of the Micronesian inhabitants. Likewise, the islanders took in the starched shorts, chalk-white legs, and pith helmet, and concluded the alien intruder was harmless but barely human. If I stepped ashore babbling in tongues, eyebrows would surely be raised at my arrival, too.

The distinguished psychologist Professor Richard P. Bentall once wrote, "It is difficult to draw up criteria for distinguishing sanity from insanity, with the ground separating [the two] so shaky." Far from being black and white, he argued, madness is a relative concept, commensurate with the tolerances of the majority and adjudicated on behalf of society by psychiatrists and judges. According to this logic, then, the same sanity that had worked for me on the ocean, the fellowship of personalities that kept me going in the countercurrent, would likely have me committed to a psychiatric hospital on land.

In short, I needed to arrive as Jason Lewis, not Heinz, the crazed U-boat commander, or a foul-mouthed Frenchman from the Monty Python series, or an unhinged IRA terrorist.

"Serge, Gary, Heinz," I said. "It's been fun travelling with you guys, but you have to go now."

"Bollix an' shoite, we're not 'goin' anywhere."

"*Oui!* Go boil your bottom, *Rosbif.*"

"*Jawohl.* Vie don't you leaf yourself Englander *schwein.*"

A choking wave of emotion welled up within me. It wasn't so much the colourful characters of an overindulgent imagination that I was letting go. It was the part of me that had been wound so tight, for so long, doing whatever it took to hold it together, even if it meant going a little crazy to avoid losing it completely. Sometimes, in the confusion and uncertainty of our daily lives, it is all we can do to just maintain. But if there is one thing we can be sure of in this world, it is that nothing is immune from change, and if we can just find a way to keep pedalling, in whatever shape or form that may take, circumstances will eventually turn in our favour.

As the boat rocked gently towards the shore, a liberating sense of exorcism spread throughout my being, and my head filled again with the sounds of the sea whispering like long-forgotten secrets trapped in a shell.

THE REPUBLIC OF KIRIBATI
THE SMILE OF A STRANGER

Doubt is a pain too lonely to know that faith is his twin brother.
—KHALIL GIBRAN

A S I ROUNDED TARAWA'S southwest point, volleys of children's laughter came ringing out across the water, breaking the spell of soporific isolation. My throat burned with thirst, and I pedalled like a drunk, my legs feeling like jelly after two sleepless nights pushing to make the all-important tide. "Cold beer, cold beer," I repeated mantra-like, squinting into the glare of the blinding lagoon.

Jake was waiting with his camera at the outer marker buoy, perched atop the bow of a large fishing vessel. Another few miles, and *Moksha* nudged up against Betio pier. An amphitheatre of brown faces greeted me as I stood up in the hatchway. They were local fishermen, their expressions neither threatening, nor approving, merely registering polite indifference. But when word spread that *Moksha* had no motor or sail, they started goggling and whispering.

Swaying gently, eyes swimming with fatigue, I nodded and smiled hello. Behind the gawking heads, a disparate panorama of greenery stretched the length of a white sandy shore, the same pristine wisp that set the scene for one of the bloodiest offensives of WWII.* The shallows were still littered with the detritus of war: rusting tanks, carpets of shell casings, and unidentifiable lumps of mollusc-encrusted metal that now served as playhouses for the kiddies frolicking in the surf.

A coconut appeared, thrust to me on the end of a bronzed, weather-beaten arm. It was ice cold—thoughtfully chilled for the occasion. I toasted the crush of now grinning faces and raised the shell to my lips. The first swig missed its mark and ran straight down my chest, but the second mouthful hit home, pouring into my belly like liquid fire. I closed my eyes in ecstasy and gulped greedily as the crowd murmured its approval.

---

* The Battle of Tarawa was the first step in a drive across the Pacific by allied forces seeking to capture airbases from which Japan could be bombed. The assault lasted 72 hours and cost the lives of 1,113 US Marines, who died retaking the three-hundred-acre landing strip at Betio. Of the 3,500 Japanese Imperial Marines defending the island, only 17 survived.

Two barefoot customs officers in wraparound shades elbowed their way forward and poked their noses into the cockpit.

"Passpot, pleez," said one, making a face like he was inspecting a dustbin. This was Eena, short and stout like his partner and his head the shape of a bowling ball. I noticed that both the men's white short-sleeved shirts were immaculately creased—a legacy of British colonial rule, I guessed.

I handed him my red booklet.

"Your last pot woz?" said Eena, slowly thumbing the pages.

"Hawaii."

"Exit stamp?"

This presented a problem. It was pointless trying to explain how my departure from Kona had fallen on a Sunday, when both immigration and customs offices had been closed, and how catching the ebb tide had been more important than pandering to the whims of officialdom's opening hours. Customs officers the world over didn't care about tides. All they cared about was the right stamp on the right bit of paper.

"The Americans, they refused to give me one," I fibbed.

Eena frowned. "Why not?"

"They thought I'd never make it to Tarawa. Thought I was a li-ability."

The sidekick signalled his disapproval by pinching the bridge of his nose between thumb and forefinger and blowing the contents onto the wharf.

I thought: *What if they refuse me entry?* The scenario of having to pedal back out to sea was unspeakably grim yet entirely possible. The more obscure and rinky-dink the country, the more anally retentive the officialdom, and Kiribati was about as obscure and rinky-dink as it got. Nobody I'd spoken to before leaving Hawaii had ever heard of the place. There was only one flight a week to and from the outside world, via Fiji, and a boat arrived once a month from Australia bringing canned food and other essentials. Starved of much if anything to do, these officials no doubt subjected Tarawa's meagre trickle of visitors to endless dawdling questions before imparting the only real power they had: the blue ink of an entry stamp. I braced myself. Going through my passport with a toothcomb was probably the highlight of Eena's week.

It was at this point that I noticed both men had their toenails painted with pink nail polish. Following the direction of my gaze, Eena coughed self-consciously, straightened himself, and handed me back my passport. "Will you come to our office Monday morning, pleez?" he asked politely. "I will stamp your passpot there."

Clearly, I was going to get along just fine in the Republic of Kiribati. In a land of burly, nail-polish-wearing officials, how could you not?

Four months later

CHRIS TIPPER HAD a guitar in one hand and a purple backpack in the other. At six foot two, the boat builder stood head and shoulders above the rest of the passengers shuffling out of Bonriki International Airport, most of them Kiribati nationals returning home from working abroad.

"I was hoping to take a month off before coming out," were the first words out of his mouth, as if picking up the conversation from where we'd left off four years ago in Colorado. "Get in shape, run around getting things we need for the voyage."

"Like what?" I enquired.

"Shark repellent, that kind of thing."

I thought of my hammer-dropping episode on the last voyage. "Oh yeah, I forgot about your shark phobia."

"Ran out of time, though. Had too many loose ends to tie up at work."

Smiling and cracking jokes, Chris looked much better than he deserved after spending thirty-six hours in a glorified cigar tube from London via LA and Fiji. His buoyant mood was also in sharp but reassuring contrast to the last time I'd seen him, vowing never to have anything to do with the expedition again.

Steve leaving the expedition offered the first opportunity to invite Chris to try out the craft that he and Hugo had built, pedalling with me to the Solomon Islands. His comic repartee would also be a welcome change from the quarrelling Continentals of the last voyage.

We crammed ourselves into one of the dangerously overladen minibuses outside the terminal, and off we went, bumping down the road towards Betio, our eardrums pounding to the blips and squeaks of a Europop song that had infected the island.

Boom boom boom boom

I want you in my room

Let's spend the night together

From now until forever

"I also brought a saxophone along," shouted Chris, patting the bag on his knee. He was perched on a narrow seat next to an enormous woman with bulging breasts who refused to budge an inch. "Thought it'd be fun to learn to play on the voyage."

I stared at him. "You didn't."

"I did."

With his characteristic deadpan expression, it was hard to know when Chris was being serious.

"Really?" I asked.

"I'm learning *Three Blind Mice* at the moment. You don't mind, do you?"

A few squealing notes played in my head. I imagined them being repeated day in, day out, with no hope of escape. "That bloody thing's going over the side as soon as we leave the harbour," I said darkly.

He laughed. "Don't worry. I didn't really bring a saxophone."

After a punishing hour at the hands of the Vengaboys (*Boom boom boom boom, I wanna double boom*), we arrived at a sky-blue bungalow on the beachfront belonging to a volunteer couple from Australia. James was a civil engineer by trade and worked as a supervisor at the Public Works Department. His wife, Joanne, practised law at the High Court. In a supreme act of humanitarian kindness, one that saved us from the infamous roaches at the overpriced Betio Motel, they'd opened their doors to the expedition for the duration of the cyclone season.

Our hosts were still at work, but a vivacious young woman with bouncing brown curls met us at the door. Annie was a producer with Video Free America in San Francisco. That morning, while I was on my way to pick up Chris, she'd been conducting a Video Exchange workshop with pupils from King George V and Elaine Bernacchi High School (KGV). Once primed with the basics of filmmaking, the teenagers were sent off to film the lives of their friends and families. The last stage was to learn how to write and record a voiceover and to edit their footage into a short film using laptops sponsored by Apple Inc. UNESCO would help distribute the finished films to schools in member countries.

Having the resources to bring in dedicated personnel had greatly advanced the expedition's core educational mission—to dispel illusory barriers between people and educate youngsters on sustainability, including how to reduce their ecological footprint—and this was just the beginning. The ultimate goal, finances permitting, was to retain a small team of professionals in the field, implementing outreach programmes in every country the expedition passed through. At the rate the stock prices were soaring on the NASDAQ, it wouldn't be long before my dream was realized.

Originally I'd hoped to carve out enough time to explore some of Tarawa's neighbouring islands where the inhabitants still lived traditionally, but with education now sharing equal billing with the circumnavigation bid, opportunities for extra curricular activities were rare.

While Annie worked on audiovisual projects, I gave presentations to schools, hung the Step Into My World photographic exhibition in the local library, distributed pen pal letters, and worked with younger children on creating photo albums for exchange.* Then there were the field trips for pupils to see *Moksha* being prepared for the upcoming voyage.

Dai Nippon Elementary was the first of several schools to visit the old storage shed at the Tarawa Technical Institute where *Moksha* was temporarily housed. Dressed neatly in magenta-and-white uniforms, the children arrived shrieking in a convoy of rusting pickups. Chris had spent the best part of the morning cleaning up after a family of rats that had taken up residence, appropriately enough, in the Rathole. When he heard the ruckus, he emerged drenched in sweat and looking tetchy, his expression saying: *You've got another thing coming if you think those bloody kids are going to clamber all over my boat!*

But the pupils turned out to be delightful, good-natured and attentive, displaying the same bonhomie extended to all *I-Matangs* (Caucasians) since the arrival of the first European sailors in the sixteenth century. The *I* in *I-Matang* means "from" in the Kiribati language, and *Matang* equates literally to "the original fatherland, the paradise sweeter than all other paradises."† The translation was shortened in English to "from the home of our ancestors," which seemed a stroke of luck. According to legend, the earliest *I-Kiribati* people were also fair-skinned.

In other words, instead of being put in a pot and eaten like they could expect to be elsewhere in the Pacific, the pasty-faced imposters had been mistaken by the locals as messengers sent from their forebears and promptly welcomed as chiefs.

---

* The pupils from Dai Nippon Elementary took the pen pal programme to another level, making their own paper using fibres extracted from coconut husks.
† *A Pattern of Islands*, Arthur Grimble.

BY MARCH 10, 2000, the technology-heavy NASDAQ had swelled to an all-time high of 5,048 points. It was a spectacular rise, more than doubling its value in one year. The expedition's nest egg had grown exponentially, the portfolio ballooning from a starting principle of $65,000 to $492,000 US dollars.

I emailed my financial advisor: *Let's cash in when the portfolio reaches half a million.*

Some news is so shocking we can remember precisely what we were doing when we first heard it: President Kennedy assassinated, the 9/11 attacks, getting dumped by a first love. At ten past three on the afternoon of March 16, I was frying an egg in James and Joanne's kitchen. Being a vegetarian on Tarawa wasn't easy. Virtually no fresh greens were grown on the island—the sandy soil was too porous and retained little moisture. The monthly supply ship brought fruits and vegetables on its meandering loop of the West Pacific, but by the time the produce got to Tarawa, much of it was old and rancid. Once the shops ran out, I survived mainly on locally supplied eggs.

Carrying my plate into the living room, I sat down at my laptop and logged into the expedition's E*trade account. *Should've reached the half-mil point by now,* I thought confidently.

Navigating to the balances section, I clicked on Net Assets.

That's strange. I peered at the figure. *Server must be down.*

I rebooted the computer and logged back in.

A bolt of red lightning streaking down to the x-axis of the equity graph said it all. Like many other investors, we'd ridden the dotcom crash all the way to the bottom. At 4:13 am Tarawa time, E*trade managers monitoring the account had liquidated the entire portfolio. In less time than it took to fry an egg, the expedition had gone bankrupt.

I left the house in a daze, walking numbly in the direction of downtown Betio to collect a printer from Mike Strubb, a Swiss expat who ran the Internet café. When he saw me he started gabbing about his

German friend, Causeway Thomas, so-called for hand-building a rock causeway to his stilted hut in the lagoon.

"It took him a year, then his Kiribati wife moved in." Mike rolled his eyes and sucked his teeth. "Her extended family moved in, too, of course. They started eating everything in sight, demanding this and that."

On any other day I would enjoy hearing one of Mike's colourful Tarawa tales, but my mind was far away.

"He couldn't get rid of them," Mike was saying, going on to recite an all too common story between *I-Matangs* and *I-Kiribatis*. According to island custom, a breadwinner couldn't turn family away, no matter how tenuous the lineage. It was the reason no one in Kiribati was rich—or starving, for that matter. Everything was shared, even money, a concept hard to grasp by Westerners. "So one day he just upped and left." Mike smiled grimly. "Now he's building another causeway further up the lagoon."

I bumped into the unfortunate German outside on the street. He was walking purposefully, blonde hair sticking out in all directions, muttering defiantly. How was the new causeway coming along, I asked?

"Ja." He nodded. "Ookay."

"Won't your wife and family just move to your new place?"

Causeway's face darkened, and he clenched his fists. "Caunts," he growled. "Zey suck, ent zey suck, ent zey suck. Focking caunts!"

On any other day I would also relish a walk through the streets of Betio at this hour. The afternoon heat had slackened, and the locals were out in droves, making for a carnival atmosphere. Three girls worked a jump rope. Two boys played ping-pong on a sheet of plywood balanced on an oil drum can, a plank of wood serving as a net. A group of young men were fixing a moped. *"Mauri!"* they called out as I passed, "Greetings." Two fat women sat behind a set of scales cradling an enormous fish crawling with flies, gossiping in ribald tones and cackling. Packs of dogs roamed for scraps, desperate things red raw with mange. A woman was washing fully clothed in front of a mirror.

But today I wasn't in the mood. Today I needed the counsel of the sea.

My mouth was parched, and my legs felt weak. The full magnitude of the catastrophe was hitting home: fifteen thousand dollars needed by the end of the month for satellite airtime, the payment on the ruggedized computer, and to compensate Annie. And where would the money come from to buy provisions for the next leg?

Stumbling down the beach, I became oblivious to where I was going anymore. The long-term picture was now dragging itself into focus: tens of thousands of miles still to go, countless more years slogging west, penniless, unable to work or fundraise in the poorer countries of Asia and Africa. *How can I carry on without money?* I thought. The whole thing suddenly seemed all too impossible. A tremendous weight bore down on my shoulders, and I sank to my knees, overcome by an irresistible urge to lie down in the sand and sleep forever. *And if I do wake up, this will all turn out to be just a bad dream ...*

Laughter roused me from my dark reverie. A young girl was sitting in the shade of a pandanus tree, sprig of white Frangipani blossom in her hair. She was smiling at me, a wide, beatific, South Pacific island smile, radiating like a lighthouse shining from an ocean of darkness. And in that moment all sense of crushing despair left me. This child had nothing, yet she was richer than Croesus, her smile alone worth more than any worldly fortune.

I knew then that as long as I caught occasional glimpses of the divine, even through the eyes of a stranger, I could persevere. Some things in this life matter too much. Things that, once you've stepped through the looking glass and realize there is no going back, you know at the core of your being are too important not to give your all. Every last effort. Every last penny. Even if it means losing all you have. And when you do—as indeed you must from time to time, in order to see what is essential but invisible to the eye—you press on regardless into the void, knowing those first rays of the morning will push back the shadows. For there is always truth if you look for it, even in the farthest-flung corners of this solitary rock we call home and the darkest recesses of the injured soul where light is seemingly absent.

Then, and only then, free of attachments and the illusion of me and the mirage of mine, can we begin to see that hope prevails because it has to. Because, in the short chapter of human history, that's all there ever was and will be, underpinning the essence of who we are, of life itself, maintaining our fragile presence on this planet. Not the flesh, blood, or the thoughts, but the primal urge of survival, the original fire, the desperate struggle against all odds in which we, the dominant species, have everything to lose and everything to gain. And we take heart, knowing the story can still turn out okay if we keep holding onto the only truly meaningful thing we ever had.

Faith.

TARAWA TO THE SOLOMONS
FINE YOUNG CANNIBALS

He just ambled from boulder to boulder, sometimes in a deliberate dance, with his legs crossing from right to left, right to left and for a while I followed his every step but then I learned it was better for me to just spontaneously pick my own boulders and make a ragged dance of my own.

—JACK KEROUAC, *The Dharma Bums*

"W E'RE AWAY, CHRIS. How do you feel, mate?"
"Relieved … Relieved and a little bit anxious. But mainly relieved."

Chris was pumping away at the pedals, a pair of black-and-white fluffy dice bobbing in front of his scarlet face. It was only mid-morning, but the temperature in the enclosed pedal seat area was already a hundred degrees. Astern, the red-and-white radio towers of Betio tapered in *Moksha's* wake, returning Tarawa to a nondescript dot on the map. Except this wasn't strictly true. Now it was a nondescript dot synonymous with myriad memories: the wonderful people we'd met, their unconditional hospitality and the general mood of live and let live, the slaphappy island life under whispering palms far from the so-called civilized world. I pulled out the chart. Eleven hundred miles to the southwest another nondescript dot was marked, more a yellow splodge: Guadalcanal, our next port of call.

An hour earlier, their noses wrinkling at the acrid stench of copra, our island friends had turned up to give us a traditional send-off from the harbour. Smiling schoolchildren lined the breakwater and waved. One of the KGV teachers, Maere, presented us with a sack of coconuts and precious cucumbers and papayas picked from her garden. Buutonga, a fifteen-year-old student who'd helped repaint *Moksha*, arrived bearing garlands of shells he and his mother had spent days painstakingly stringing together.

Then there was Brendan, an Australian. He winked and slipped us each a packet of condoms. "You boys might need them for the voyage. Go easy on each other, eh?"

Indeed, one of the most traditional farewells came from a fellow Aussie.

"Take a look at this," I said to Chris as we slipped out of the harbour entrance. "The moon rising over Betio."

At the end of the wharf, a pair of chalky buttocks gleamed. They belonged to our illustrious host, James, tucked in a time-honoured

Down Under salute. The poor sod was clearly delighted to finally see the back of us and reclaim his home.

This base spectacle pretty much set the tone for the voyage. Part way into his first break, Chris stood up and made an announcement.

"I'm gonna go for my first poo. Hopefully. I'm a little bit tensed up, though, so it might be a bit of a squeeze. But, yeah, it's nice to be putting something back into the ocean."

I had the camera rolling. "Okay. Away you go."

"So, do you take your underpants off before you get out there?"

"It'll be quite messy if you don't."

"But that means I'll be naked in front of you."

"Yup, in front of the whole world. You're live on the Internet, luvvy."

Chris hesitated for a moment, deliberating. "Tell you what. I'll try keeping my pants on first, 'cos I'm that kind of guy."

"That's very modest of you."

"Well, it's all different, isn't it?"

"You'll get used to it."

"No toilet paper, either." He puckered his mouth and grimaced. "Still, I've never had a view this nice from me bog before."

Relieved of this information, he clambered onto the starboard gunwale, wrestled off his boxer shorts, and squatted next to the pedal seat. His bare arse was just inches away through the Perspex.

"You don't have to do it beside me," I protested.

"Where can I go then?"

"Go wherever you want." I gestured to the front hatch. "Hang on to that rail up there."

"Which rail?"

"On the front compartment."

"Oh, the front compartment."

Shuffling forward, he crouched down again, tipping *Moksha* to starboard.

"Give us a wave," I hollered, zooming in.

The silhouette of a hand wagged back and forth in the viewfinder.

I cackled with delight. "That's the victory wave, that is. Bombs successfully away!"

Next morning, the wisecracks came to a screeching halt when my crewmate turned pale and lunged for the side.

"That's ten quid you owe me," I said, watching the pancake breakfast splatter into the drink. Gloating over the outcome of a bet as to who would be the first to throw up wasn't usually my style, but Chris was rather stuck on his own sense of seamanship.

He groaned, wiped his mouth with the back of his hand, and flopped back against the passenger seat. "It's your bloody cooking, Lewis."

"What do you mean *your bloody cooking?* You're just a sorry landlubber, Mr Tipper. And a sore loser."

He glowered at me. "That pancake mix you cooked with—"

"What about it?"

"It's rancid. Got weevils in it."

"Nonsense."

"Look for yourself."

I did and saw that he was right. Dotted throughout the Ziploc bag were dozens of white grubs, each about a centimetre long, their pale colour rendering them barely distinguishable from the surrounding powder. This, I knew, signalled trouble. Chris was famously fussy about his food. The distinct possibility that our entire supply of pancake mix was infested with weevil larvae would go down like a lead balloon.

"Never mind," I offered optimistically. "We've still got porridge oats."

But Chris wasn't having it. "Why didn't you check the food before we left?"

The truth was I'd been afraid to. Paid for with the hasty sale of a laptop and one of the Video Exchange cameras, all of our provisions were substandard. The store in Betio had brought in a special order of veggies—carrots, cabbages, onions, and garlic—but the stuff was half rotten before we'd even stowed it. Even more worrying were the canned goods: soup, sweet corn, kidney beans, spaghetti in tomato sauce, mushrooms in brine, mandarin oranges, peanut butter, and the like. It was the same brand of Australian budget fodder, processed and packed with preservatives in drab yellow tins, allegedly responsible for more than seventy per cent of Kiribati adults being classified as obese and over half the population suffering from diabetes, many requiring limb amputations.*

The atrocious food threatened to sabotage life on *Moksha*, too. The more Chris complained, the more his griping got under my skin. Finally, I found a light-hearted way of pointing out that at least we had something to eat.

PLACING MY FEET either side of the cockpit, I gripped the wind generator pole with one hand and reached up to retrieve a sweat-encrusted towel drying on the front shroud with the other. I was about to climb down when I felt a sharp, stabbing pain in my scrotum.

"Forty fifteen!" Chris crowed triumphantly. "Match point."

We were a week into the voyage. Planting a clothes peg on a pair of exposed gonads was puerile in the extreme, but kept us endlessly entertained with games of Testicle Tennis. And since neither of us had worn a stitch since our first day out from Tarawa, the pace of play was brisk.

"That's cheating," I replied angrily. "You asked me to pass you your towel."

"Tough titties, Lewis. You should have been more on the ball—no pun intended."

---

* In just a few decades, the traditional Tarawa diet comprising largely of fish and co-conuts has been replaced by fat-laden, processed foods imported from elsewhere (Spam being a favourite). For metabolisms adapted to endure lean times by converting any spare calories to fat, the change in diet has proved disastrous.

At the next shift change, Chris, who was as fastidious about personal hygiene as he was with his food, decided to have a wash and a shave. He leaned over the side and began cropping his goatee with a beard trimmer.

"I like to have a shave every once in a while," he noted casually, thrusting his chin towards the small travel mirror he was holding. "It makes me feel like I'm, err—"

"A real man?" I volunteered.

"Well, yeah, it makes me feel like a real man." He stopped shaving and gazed out to sea with knowing assurance. "Makes me feel like I'm in control."

"So you're a control freak then, Chris?"

He turned to me straight-faced. "Ay? No, it makes me feel like I'm on patrol."

"On patrol? So you really want to be in the army."

"Yeah, I'm a patrol freak!"

"I think you've signed up for the wrong programme, mate."

Such episodes of verbal sparring were invaluable. As well as keeping the atmosphere light, humorous interplay offered a non-confrontational way of handling potentially explosive issues: the dreadful food, whose turn it was to write an update for the website, whether the other guy was sneaking extra Cliff Bars during his graveyard shift, and so forth. As Steve and I had found out the hard way on the Atlantic, it was crucial to allow another human being the opportunity to save face living in such close proximity.

"I tell you, it's a right laugh here, innit," said Chris, reaching for one of the pint-sized Tupperware containers. "I'm gonna go and have a shower, next."

I was filming again. "Shall we come with you?"

He motioned with his head. "Come on, then." Climbing out onto the port gunwale, he placed the receptacle over his penis and slipped into an Aussie accent: "Gotta do the decent thing here and cover up me proivates." He worked his way aft, hanging onto the rail with both hands. "Look at that! You can tell I've been on board for a few days, can't ya?"

"Very impressive," I conceded, genuinely mystified at how the container was staying in place all by itself.

Sitting across the stern deck, Chris proceeded to douse himself, scooping with the cup and flinging seawater over his head.

"I'm gonna turn the shower on really fast now." He worked the container faster and faster. "It's really coming out the nozzle." Fortunately, it was a calm day and the chances of falling overboard were slim. "Blimey," he exclaimed, "doesn't anyone know there's a water shortage out here?"

Together with regular doses of comedy, the peaceable ambience was helped by near idyllic conditions. The wind blew a steady ten knots from the northeast, and most days we notched an easy sixty to sixty-five miles in spite of the heat. If we were lucky, a squall blustered across our path, washing away a fetid stagnancy that grew like mildew in our cramped quarters.

We swam only once, on the afternoon of day ten. Donning goggles, we slipped over the side, peering anxiously for anything that resembled a darting fin or slinking shadow. Far below us, a vast shoal of glinting fish fanned out in all directions, their bodies flitting back and forth like perfectly synchronized shutter blinds turning the limpid depths from dark to light, then light to dark.

That evening, as Chris strummed his guitar out on deck, the same abundance of life broke the surface in a breathtaking explosion of animation. A million chinks of silver churned the water to the horizon, filling the air with the deafening roar of a river in flood.

Then, as quickly as they'd appeared, the fish were gone.

June 8

"JUST GOT AN email through from the old man about the situation on Guadalcanal." I was examining the laptop wedged between my knees. "Looks like there's been a coup. 'Current advice is not, repeat not, to come to Honiara. Fighting is continuing just outside the airport. Air links are tenuous. Tulagi and the Florida Islands will be the next safe port of call. It is impossible to say what the security situation will be like in a week's time. It is changing daily'."

This altered everything. It was bad enough trying to outwit the intricacies of currents, winds, and seasonal weather fluctuations in our bid to raise the next yellow splodge on the map, but the human factor, something we hadn't really had to contend with until now, put a completely different spin on things.

"What if I can't leave?" Chris voiced uneasily, a reminder that he needed to get back to his business.

Plus there was the added logistical conundrum of April. Having first travelled with the expedition four years earlier from Colorado to San Francisco, the schoolteacher was due to arrive in Honiara in twelve days' time to accompany me on the final leg of the Pacific. All three of us couldn't possibly ride in *Moksha* all the way to Australia.

"Mind you," I pointed out, "if you can't fly out, I doubt whether April will be able to fly in. You may be pedalling with me to Australia whether you like it or not."

The situation deteriorated over the following days. The airport closed. Five Malaitans died when Guadalcanal militants fired on their boat with a bazooka. And in the most grisly incident of all, a decapitated body was dumped in the market outside Honiara.

Somewhat predictably given the history of tit for tat headhunting expeditions throughout the region, the conflict had reignited centuries-old feuds between the people of Malaita and their Guadalcanal rivals, offering a chance to settle old scores. Except this latest spat had actually been instigated by foreigners. Brought to Guadalcanal by American forces in 1942, business-savvy Malaitans had stayed on after the war, taking the best jobs, buying up the best land, and sowing the seeds of future resentment with the more sedentary indigenous population.

As we neared the northern tip of Malaita, Chris and I began taking a daily dose of doxycycline as a prophylactic against malaria. According to David Stanley writing for *Lonely Planet*, the Solomon Islands was one of the best places in the world to study the disease owing to ninety-eight per cent of the inhabitants being infected with it.

"Most common place to get bitten is on the ankles, apparently." Chris was reading from the Papua New Guinea and Solomon Islands edition of the guidebook series while eating a bowl of porridge laced with dried fruits, nuts, and weevils. "Between seven and eight, Monday through Friday."

Stanley also described the Malaitans as "cantankerous, wary of outsiders," and, until the beginning of the last century, known for "regularly cooking and eating shipwrecked sailors."

Chris flicked the page. "Sounds like a friendly enough place."

"We should roll up as we are," I suggested from the pedal seat. "Naked. That way they can see how skinny we are. Not much to eat."

"Yeah. If you see a big pot on the beach with steaming water in it, you know it's not a hot tub."

Chris went on to relate various other local eccentricities. These included worshiping sharks (the people believed them to embody the spirits of their dead ancestors) and Marching Rule, a cargo cult established by islanders invoking the same airdrops they saw raining down on Allied troops in WWII. Even the lingua franca of Solomons Pidgin sounded fantastically kooky. Bra translated as *basket bilong titi.* Helicopter was *mixmaster bilong Jesus Christ.* And the most supremely satisfying of them all, piano, came out as *one big fella black box, him he got black teeth, him he got white teeth, you strike him hard, him cry out.*

That such a wonderfully quirky, idiosyncratic place still existed in an increasingly bland and homogenized world thrilled the pair of us. We couldn't wait to get there.

Monday, June 19
THE BIRD FIRST appeared as a black speck against the florid canvas of the west, tacking into a light headwind. As the shape steadily grew, the bent wings and deeply forked tail left us in no doubt: a frigatebird, heading doggedly back to land as such birds are said to do at evening time.

The same scene of a black frigatebird set against a ruddy sunset was painted either side of *Moksha's* bow. Before leaving Kiribati, I'd recruited the art teacher at KGV, a quiet, self-effacing man named Karawa, to update the spirit guide that had brought the boat safely across the East Pacific.* The old Gilbertese sailing hands who Karawa had consulted proposed a frigatebird, considered auspicious in Melanesian seafaring lore for guiding sailors to the safety of land.

A short while later, a shout rang out from the foredeck.

"Oi think oi can smell land, skipper!" Chris was inhaling great wooffulls of air through his voluminous nostrils and thundering in piratese. "Oi think it's a farmyard, skipper!"

I replied that it was more likely to be the inside of the boat that he smelt. Then I noticed a telltale mass of white cumulus lingering on the southern horizon. Beneath it, our man-eater island lay hidden.

As night fell, we tracked silently along the north shore, aiming for the narrow channel separating Malaita from its satellite islet of Mbathakana. An explosion of ragged heads took shape in the moonlight—coconut palms, their starburst silhouettes bowing in deference

---

* The first guide was a sacred raven designed by a Native American artist, Jason Lacy, from the seafaring Quinault Nation in British Columbia.

to a ribbon of ivory sand that rumbled and sighed under the booming surf. Snatches of damp earth and cooking fires came wafting to us on the offshore breeze, hinting evocatively at the villages concealed in the darkness beyond.

Standing in the open cockpit, I bent down and said in a hushed voice, "Just think of that island being infested with cannibals, Chris."

The shipwright stopped pedalling and joined me to witness the Robinson Crusoe moment. A necklace of dark, velvety clouds, their bruised bellies swollen with rain, ringed the island's higher elevations. To the southwest, falling from space like a diamond dagger, the Southern Cross had pierced the edge of the farthermost cloudbank. Astern, the moon was a day on the wane from its whole self, sending a wedge of cheddar light bouncing across the water.

"Fuuucckk," whispered Chris.

"Not so long ago it would have been as well."

"I know. Mad isn't it?"

"Imagine all those buggers coming out in their war canoes."

But Chris wasn't listening anymore. He was back in the pedal seat, cranking away. "I'm gonna sort of ... head out that way a bit, I think."

Moksha veered to starboard, taking us farther out to sea.

A HORDE OF coffee-coloured urchins in dugouts swarmed out to meet us. They were earthen and shirtless with mad frizzy hair, not an ounce of fat on their pinched, wiry torsos. Sitting with knees folded to their chests in the bottom of crudely carved boats that wobbled alarmingly, the rug rats of Auki ran rings around *Moksha*, zipping to and fro with the wilful agility of a cloud of gnats. In the distance, behind a sullen drape of trees, stilted huts fashioned from the forest looked like they'd been there a thousand years—which they probably had. Cockerels crowed in the dusty shadows, and invisible drums pounded out a tattoo, making the hairs on the back of my neck stand up.

Tah-duh-duh ... Tah-duh-duh ... Tah-duh-duh ...

What an utterly unique entry into a magical land, I thought. Arriving at an airport, railway station, even a seaport ensured for the most part the same mundane experience wherever you went in the world circa 2000: dreary officials, uninspiring fast food franchises, glassy-eyed chauffeurs clutching scraps of cardboard marked *Arthur Ellis Pty Ltd,* and so on. Such sterile introductions afforded little if any insight into the heart and soul of a country and its people. By contrast, arriving in *Moksha* in the arse end of nowhere, buck naked and by the grace of human power, provided about as authentic an initiation as could be had.

"Is your canoe any good?" I asked the nearest waif, signalling to the blue-stained boat he was paddling that looked set to tip over at any moment. This was Alphones, twelve perhaps, his sun-scorched Afro streaked with natural highlights. He wore Adidas sweatpants and spoke a little English.

"Yess," he hissed. "Fairy gud."

"Fast?"

"Yess. Fairy fass."

His canoe bucked and weaved and water slopped over the side.

"Bet ours is faster," I challenged.

Alphones looked at me and grinned, revealing a set of pearly teeth. "Noo. We beat you *tumas.*"

"Rubbish." I laughed, looking to egg him on. "Fancy a race?"

He beat us easily, of course, despite Chris pedalling for all he was worth. Alphones and his friends then escorted us to a dilapidated wooden pier obscured by a large, steel-sided passenger ferry, the Ramus II, billowing evil black soot.

We'd opted at the last minute to stop off in Auki, twenty-five miles down the west coast of Malaita, to clear immigration and get the latest on the security situation. It had taken all day pedalling against a deceptively strong current, time slowing to an agonizing dawdle as our eagerness to make landfall mounted, the sight of columns of smoke rising from the jungle a mile off our port beam only compounding our impatience. Arriving outside the lagoon entrance with less than half an hour of daylight remaining and no adequate chart, we'd decided to wait, taking it in turns to hold our position through the night, before navigating the last few miles in the morning.

As we squeezed in behind the Ramus II, hundreds of prying heads gathered on the wharf above us, displaying every hair style, colour, and skin tone imaginable: the coal-black face of a scowling man from Bougainville Province here, the horrified expression of an albino there. Chris threw the painter to a teenager with the reggae look down to a T: fake designer shades, shoulder-length dreads, and marijuana leaf depicted on his shirt. Another Bob Marley devotee watched idly from the sidelines, the sweltering fabric of his wool beanie dyed the Rastafarian colours of red, yellow, and green.

Many of the people were disembarking refugees from Guadalcanal, wild-eyed and traumatized by the fighting. Some jostled and gawked. Others bared their teeth, black gums showing horribly. Were they smiling? It was hard to tell. Perhaps David Stanley was right: Malaitains were indeed cantankerous all the time, with or without regional disputes. And where were the women? Looking up at the faces, all of which belonged to men, I noticed another common trait, one that sent a chill through me. Smeared around every mouth and staining every set of purplish lips was fresh blood. Even their teeth were streaked with it.

Recalling our banter about hot tubs, I nudged Chris and cocked my eyebrows at the wall of ghoulish expressions.

"Betel nut," he muttered.

"Huh?"

"Betel. That's what they're chewing."

The penny dropped. The habit of mixing the areca nut with betel leaf and lime was widespread throughout Oceania, producing a foamy red residue and mild euphoria when chewed.

A big man in a pork pie hat, his shirt streaked with betel juice, barged to the front. "You comin' from where?" he demanded.

"Tarawa," I replied, trying not to look as alarmed as I felt.

Big Man frowned. He hadn't heard of Tarawa. Hacking a gob of crimson slime onto the wharf, he glared suspiciously at us. "From Guadalcanal?"

Chris gestured to the north. "No. Kiribati. But originally from England."

A flicker of recognition. "Motor?"

"No motor."

"Sail?"

"No sail. Human power."

Big Man had no idea what Chris was talking about. To better explain, Chris unlatched the pedal unit, lifted it onto the roof of the cockpit, and spun the propeller. "Like a bicycle, see?"

A low murmur rippled through the crowd.

"Let me see dis," said Big Man, taking the unit.

Using the utmost caution, as if the strange contraption might go off in his hands at any moment, Big Man examined the propeller, shaft, pedals, and the collar that locked it all down to the stainless steel box. He worked the cranks, shaking his head as the propeller turned. Finally, his disbelieving gaze came to the inscription that Scott Morrison had hammered into the casing.

"What dis?" he asked, tracing a giant finger over the immortal words.

"That's the name of the pedal unit," replied Chris. "'Cos it's the dog's bollocks."

Big Man grimaced. "Da what?"

"The … Never mind. It's the motor."

"Look deez men." Big Man turned to the crowd and held the unit above his head. "Dey use dis comin' awl the way from England to Auki. No gazoline!"

The people swayed and groaned, and for a second I thought they were all going to fall to their knees and start worshiping The Dog's Bollocks. Big Man then handed the unit back to Chris, smiled a broad, betel-stained smile, and said, "Plees, you are both fairy welcome to Malaita."

And with that, Chris and I clambered onto the pier, and the crowd, still whispering and murmuring, parted like the Red Sea, allowing us to take our first tentative steps into the realm of the so-called Happy Isles.

EXCEPT WITH THE oil close to running out, the economy in free fall, and shops running out of food, the situation in the Solomon Islands was anything but happy.* The old timers simply went back to growing taro in their gardens, but the younger generation, weaned on a money economy, loafed around aimlessly like exiles in their own land. Only the churches and money changers seemed to be doing well out of the crisis.

An Australian war journalist and his local stringer were nosing around for stories. Otherwise, we were the only outsiders in Auki—all the expats had been evacuated. A general air of despondency greeted us as we stumbled punch drunk through the dusty streets in the direction of the police station, our first port of call to see if we could clear immigration. An inquisitive crowd followed, asking a barrage of questions.

"What about da rough sea?"

"Any sea monsters?"

---

* No supply tanker would come near the place for fear of being hijacked by militia.

"This expedition is very interesting. We haven't seen anything like this before in Auki."

A sweating man labouring under an assortment of woodcarvings blocked our way, looking desperate. "Where you from? Where you going? When you leaving?" He shook a salad bowl in my face. I shook my head in reply. A salad bowl would find scant use aboard *Moksha*. Besides, we needed to conserve what little money we had left for buying supplies to reach Australia.

I told him as much.

"But I need food for my family," he protested.

At the police station, we introduced ourselves to the two officers on duty, George and Basil.

"Come back at nine," said Basil upon hearing our request. "The line to Honiara is cut."

It was eight. We went away, changed a little money at the Chinese store, and chanced upon a bakery selling frosted buns.

"Just coconut sprinkled on freshly baked rolls," said Chris, pushing the better part of a whole bun into his mouth. "Tastes fantastic, though."

At nine, we returned to the police station. We were told to come back at eleven. At eleven, we were told to come back at two. All we could do was shrug, smile politely, and comply. If we got shirty, likely we would end up waiting even longer.

At two, the police chief, a tall man with greying hair, ushered us into his office. A sign on the wall listed three directives to be a better policeman: Distinguish Sense from Nonsense, Learn to Listen, and Learn the Facts. His desk had four trays on it marked In, Out, Pending, and Action. They were all empty.

"The line to Honiara is still cut, I'm afraid." The chief made a convincing job of sounding resigned, but a ballpoint twirling happily up and down his fingers told another story. "We also tried contacting them by radio, but there was no response." Leaning over his desk, he pursed his lips at us in feigned sympathy. "I am sorry, my friends, but you cannot stay in Auki. You will need to leave for Tulagi as soon as possible."

This seemed harsh. Pedalling away without even washing off the salt wasn't quite the reception we'd been hoping for. A magical solution then came to me. "I've got an idea. You could use our satellite phone to call them!"

The chief made jibbing noises and stabbed the air with his pen. Clearly, he had no intention of making contact with his superiors on Guadalcanal. As long as the line remained cut, he would continue to enjoy full autonomy of his little fiefdom and have a nice holiday to boot. A satellite call would ruin all of that.

In the end, citing mechanical difficulties, unfavourable tides, and the wrath of Her Majesty Queen Elizabeth II should we drown en route, Chris and I managed to negotiate a 48-hour layover. Leaving Alphones and his friend Calvin to keep an eye on *Moksha*, we booked in for a night at the Auki Motel, a yellow brick affair filled with excitable young men who turned out to be fighters with the Malaita Eagle Force (MEF). They were awaiting orders to ship out to Guadalcanal.

One insisted on showing us his gun. Ushering us into a room, he reached under the bed and pulled out a yellow dry bag containing an AK47.

"I have many guns," he boasted, snapping the magazine in place. "I am commander."

This seemed unlikely. He looked about ten.

"Where did you receive your training?" Chris asked doubtfully.

The boy tapped the side of his head. "Awl in 'ere."

Making our excuses, we hurried off to meet George the policeman at the Auki Lodge, side-stepping Bowl Man who was waiting in ambush. As a thank you for guarding *Moksha* overnight ("Adults, they won't touch it," George had warned, "but the children, they may take things"), we'd invited him to dinner. There was only one item on the menu, a dull-tasting omelette served with rice costing fifty-three Solomon dollars for three portions. Tourist price.

When I returned from the boat with more cash, Chris was engaged in a spirited conversation with another MEF soldier, Paul, well on his way to oblivion at the hands of the local palm wine known throughout the Pacific as *arrack.* The two were getting along famously, laughing and carrying on, demonstrating how easy it is to make friends wherever you are, regardless of language or cultural impediment, if your knowledge of one particular topic is up to scratch.

Soccer.

England had just beaten Germany one-nil in the European Championships.

WE SLIPPED OUT of Auki in darkness on the evening of the second day. A crowd had gathered on the wharf to bid us bon voyage. George and Basil were there, along with Paul, nursing a hangover, the rest of the MEF fighters from the Auki Motel, and a friendly furniture maker from Papua New Guinea called Eekai. A solitary light bulb at the end of the pier illuminated a sea of hands held aloft.

"Thanks, Malaita," Chris called out, waving as I pedalled. "Be lucky."

The last goodbyes faded, and we pushed into the night, accompanied by a flotilla of splashing dugouts led by Alphones. When we reached the harbour limits, they, too, melted away.

"Special place," I said.

"Yeah," Chris agreed, reaching inside the Rathole for his shell jacket. The wind had freshened from the northeast, whipping the waves and sending water into the cockpit. "Really good people. It's just not true what you read in the books—as far as I'm concerned. Malaitans, a fantastic bunch."

In spite of the oil running out, the fear, uncertainty, and skyrocketing cost of a pound of rice, the people of Auki had taken us in, embraced us like family and protected us, reinforcing in my mind a growing truism of travel, that the places others tell you to avoid often turn out to be the best-kept secrets.

THE GREEN HILLS of Siota emerged from the morning mist like the South Dorset coast rising up from Chesil Beach, a view I hadn't laid eyes on in six long years. Drawing closer, it became apparent that parcels of ground had been cleared to grow food during the troubles, a necessary pragmatism that gave the island a worn, moth-eaten look, calling to mind the scrawny heathlands of the Purbeck Peninsula. Then the trademark white sandy shore studded with palm trees became visible, putting me firmly back in the tropics.

While I sat on the foredeck watching for rocks, Chris steered carefully into the mouth of the Mboli Passage, a channel of brackish water offering a shortcut to Tulagi by going through, not around, the Nggela islands. The throat quickly narrowed, sandwiching us between twitching tendrils of rioting foliage and filling our lungs with the damp, musty smells of virgin rainforest. An orgy of competing sounds closed in, a rich cacophony of jungle mayhem, feral and savage, conjuring images of Mr Kurtz lying wracked in fever at the Heart of Darkness, his sanity blown.

"I'd love to see a crocodile," said Chris.

I looked at him. "Are you sure?"

"Yeah, well"—he wrinkled his nose—"it's not going to tip this thing over, is it?"

A cluster of grass huts appeared on the east bank. As we drew level, a squadron of dugouts struck out from shore to intercept us. They were fishermen, friendly as it turned out, though apparently unaccustomed to seeing pedal boats on the river. Tying their canoes in a long tail to *Moksha's* stern, they climbed aboard, fourteen in total, chattering and laughing and shamelessly inquisitive.

Standing on the gunwales, our guests took it in turns to strum Chris's guitar and ask the by now customary questions: Where you from? Where you go? Where da motor?

Chris showed them, pulling the unit out and spinning the propeller. "Simple," he said, grinning. "Good, isn't it?"

One with glassy eyes and bushy hair lounged on the foredeck in a *Cleveland, USA* wife-beater. "How long … you take from … Kiribati to Solomons?" he asked, cannabis cigarette dancing in his mouth.

"Twenty-one days," I replied.

He squinted at me through the smoke. "And from Honiara now … you are … heading for somewhere?"

"Cairns, Australia."

"Ah, okay."

Satisfied with my answers, he reached for the guitar and tried a few chords, but quickly abandoned the effort—too stoned to continue. One of his friends said something rude and they all laughed.

"Aargh … I tone know dis bloody ting."

And all the while the men were yakking at each other in their mother tongue, firing short, animated bursts punctuated with glottal stops. The dialect sounded almost Arabic, sentences suffused with suppressed drama, rising and falling as in song.

Chris leaned over and tapped one of the dugouts. "Mahogany?"

The owner shook his head.

"What's the name of this wood?" Chris asked.

The man thought for a moment, and then said, "Apkwa."

"Apkwa," Chris repeated.

The fisherman laid his hands on *Moksha*. "What is dis made of?"

"Plywood," replied Chris, patting the superstructure. "And this." He reached down to the hull. "This is cedar and cachimbo."

Moksha was sagging dangerously under the weight, water spewing over the stainless steel box holding The Dog's Bollocks.

"Jase," Chris said. "We're going to have to ask some of these guys to leave."

Only Peter remained, a nine year old with navy blue shorts and a yellow satchel fashioned from an old rice sack slung around his neck.

"My brudda," said one of the men before casting off, "he can go wid you to his village?" He waved downstream. "Is okay?"

"No problem," I said.

Making fast his dugout to the port side cleat, the young Florida Islander made his way forward and perched on the bow like a resting bird, snatching anxious glances at us. To put our guest at ease, Chris offered him the last of the frosted buns from the Hot Bread Bakery in Auki. Peter looked at the pastry in horror, as if it might be poisoned. Then, in an endearing act of diplomacy, he picked the offending article up between thumb and forefinger, and popped it in his satchel to dispose of later.

When I gave him the guitar to play, he took it eagerly. *Perhaps if I sing, these white devils won't eat me!* Strumming lightly at first, the boy began whispering a missionary hymn, gulping with nervousness. After swallowing the first verse, his second stanza came stronger, the third stronger still, and soon Peter's mellifluous tones filled the air with such sweet resonance that Chris and I found ourselves transported by the moment. There we were, lost in the South Pacific, gliding along some wild, untamed waterway being serenaded by this dusky island child, birds wheeling in to roost for the night and the sun slanting low, setting the western sky ablaze in a feverish tapestry of light.

Solomons to Australia
Coral Sea Cowgirl

For as this appalling ocean surrounds the verdant land, so in the soul of man there lies one insular Tahiti, full of peace and joy, but encompassed by all the horrors of the half known life. God keep thee! Push not off from that isle, thou canst never return!

—HERMAN MELVILLE, *MOBY DICK*

C HRIS AND I SAT in the restaurant at Vanita's, the only guest
house on Tulagi, supping beers and reflecting on the voyage.
This being the Solomon Islands, the establishment was blessed
with a modicum of the surreal: the same ABBA tape looped 24/7,
croaking frogs marched across the tables at mealtimes, and Betty, the
server, brought coffee half an hour after you asked for tea and collapsed
into fits of gappy-toothed giggles if you even looked at her.

Leaning across the cane table, Chris adopted a confessionary tone.
"Jase, there's something I didn't tell you before we left Tarawa."

After living in each other's pockets for a month, there weren't many
secrets left between us.

"Go on," I said.

"On my way out from England, I almost got cold feet and turned
back from LA."

He went on to describe how, in his early twenties, he'd crewed on a
three-masted barque sailing from England to Spain. In the middle of
the night, a gale blew up in the busy shipping lanes off Dover. Before
the nine-person crew had time to shorten sail, a series of sixty-knot
gusts had shredded the canvas. The paraffin navigation lights blinked
and died. The homespun hulk then turned on her beam-ends and began listing, submerging the leeward deck and flooding the sole boards
in the cabins. With no engine, the ninety-foot square-rigger was a sitting
duck. Hundred-thousand-tonne container ships were bearing down on
them in the darkness.

Chris took a pull from his bottle of SolBrew and shuddered. "I was
convinced we were all going down with the ship. Ever since then I've
been—how should I say it—rather intimidated by large bodies of untamed water."

Listening to his terrifying ordeal, I felt a pang of guilt and of admiration. The very thing I loved, the sea, had been his nemesis. Unaware
of the irony (he was a boat builder, after all), I'd taunted him merci-

lessly throughout the voyage, joking about sharks, crocodiles, squalls, lightning, even swimming. It was the same clumsy teasing he'd borne at the hands of his friends before leaving Brighton: *Chris, did you remember the shark repellent, mate?* Yet, in spite of all this leg pulling, he'd confronted his crippling fear of the sea by surrendering to the whims of a tiny boat bobbing across the Pacific.

"I feel like I've been cured," he said softly, studying the lush, green islands to the north. Then, in a rare allusion to the boat-building debacle in 1994, he added, "And suitably rewarded, too."

July 3, 2000. Coral Sea departure
"So, WHAT DO ye think life aboard *Moksha* will be like?" asked Kenny from behind his camera.

April considered this for a moment, letting her gaze drop to the heavy torpor of the harbour water. It was a stock question for a documentary filmmaker to ask, one that allowed any preconceived notions of an undertaking to be juxtaposed with the reality of it during the editing process. And for April, a middle-aged mother and teacher from Colorado, it was particularly poignant. She'd never been in a boat before, let alone to sea. She could swim none too well, either.

"I think life on the boat will be interesting," April replied hesitantly. She was sitting on a fractured slab of concrete, part of the old wharf at the National Fisheries Development Company on Tulagi. "All of a sudden my world is going to rock. The cooking is going to be a bit different. Washing clothes. Going to the bathroom. Washing my hair. And it's all with saltwater. So, I kinda wonder if I'm going to feel like a pickled herring by the time these next four weeks are over."

Earlier that day, she and Kenny had made it to Honiara on the first flight from Port Moresby in over a month. A lull in fighting had allowed the Air Niugini plane to stay on the ground long enough to discharge its human cargo and pick up a fresh load, Chris included, before taking off again. Just in time, apparently. As the pair boarded a ferry to the relative safety of the Florida Islands, word came through of a hostile force advancing on the airport, spearheaded by a homemade tank. Someone with creative flair and a socket set had bolted half-inch steel plate to the sides of a D8 bulldozer, and mounted a .50 calibre Browning machine gun disinterred from a WWII ammunition dump to the cab roof.

"Are ye afraid ay anythin'?"

April smiled. "I'm pretty much open to it all. I don't know what to fear, so I don't fear anything at this point."

One week later

WE SLIPPED THE lines at first light.

"Goodbye, everybody," I said, shoving *Moksha* away from the dock with my foot.

A handful of early shift workers from the fish depot had gathered to gawp. "Goot-byeee," answered one, his eyes popping at what he was seeing. *No motor? No sail? All the way to Australia?* "Dispela boi bagarapim het," he mumbled to his friends. This bloke must be buggered in the head.

April and I had spent the week readying for the final push to Australia: scrubbing corrosion from metal fittings, lubricating moving parts, and stowing locally sourced provisions. A few modifications to the boat were also needed, including a magnifying lens secured to a spatula in front of the compass, allowing April to better read the degree markers. In the event I disappeared overboard, she received a crash course in navigation and proper use of a lifejacket, flares, and one of the RAF rescue mirrors to signal aircraft.

By the eighth morning, it was time to get going before the Southeast

Trades blew any stronger or the local security situation deteriorated. April steered out from behind the *Arctic Wolf,* a hulking factory ship loaded with frozen tuna, and aimed for the mist-drenched shores of Nggela Sule. Before us, the tranquil waters mirrored the swollen pinks of another tropical dawn.

"Hang oot there fer a minute, will ye?" Kenny's voice barked over the radio. "I'll jis' get ay few still shots."

A minute later, he had what he wanted, and we were free to get on with the voyage.

"So where are we headed again?" asked April, peering through the forward window.

"Australia," I replied.

She rolled her eyes. "I know that!"

"Turn to starboard. Then head due south."

This would take us across The Slot, the deep-water channel between Guadalcanal and the Florida Islands. It had rained during the night, leaving traces of damp, empty silence, a sober contrast to the bedlam that raged for two days in November 1942. By the end of the Naval Battle of Guadalcanal, more than forty Allied and Japanese warships littered the ocean floor, giving it the nickname Iron Bottom Sound.

Wearing a black sports top, khaki shorts, and sandals, April looked primed for adventure. I had a fair idea of what was going through her head. She was already out on the high seas, skin flecked with salt and the wind whipping her hair, reliving the maverick life of her pirate heroine, Anne Bonny.

She giggled and held up her wrists to show off a pair of blue canvas straps. "I've got my seasickness bands on, so I'm set."*

I nodded. "And for the next month you can eat as much as you like, twenty-four hours a day."

"And not get fat?"

---

* These act on a pressure point in the wrist.

"And not get fat."

She chuckled some more and hunched her shoulders at the thought. *"Moksha,* the ultimate in weight-loss programmes. I love this!"

Skirting the southern edge of Tulagi, a white speedboat flying the red flag of the Malaita Eagle Force hove into view. The name on the bow intimated this was *Gary's Pride,* manned by two scruffy-looking men in army fatigues standing behind a tinted windscreen. A third, his forest green tee shirt crossed with ammunition belts, slouched on the foredeck. He held his semi-automatic Rambo-style: propped carelessly against his hip at forty-five degrees.

I was on the satellite phone doing an interview with Chris Court, our old friend with the UK Press Association. "Chris, I'll have to call you back." I ducked inside the cabin. "We've got company."

While April continued to pedal, I stashed the cameras, sat phone, and laptop out of sight. On Tulagi we'd heard of yachts and power-boats being stripped of their electronics by roving bands of militia, in some cases the vessels commandeered outright. *Gary's Pride* was clearly a case in point. The craft had almost certainly been stolen from one of the marinas in Honiara. The likelihood of any of these thugs be-ing called Gary or having a certificate of boat ownership struck me as remote.

The helmsman cut the engine, and they rocked towards us in the swell. "Holim!" one of them shouted. "Stap."

April quit pedalling while I stood up and waved. All I had on was a yellow lava-lava with green palm trees and The Republic of Kiribati printed in bold letters. Seconds passed. Nobody spoke. The gun-toting Rambo on the foredeck sized *Moksha* up while I grinned my head off. In contrast to our low-tech crossing of the Atlantic, the boat now bristled with antennas: VHF radio whip, mushroom-shaped transceivers for the satellite phone, Inmarsat-C, and Collision Avoidance Radar Detector, the Ocean Sentry stick, and Varigas reflector ball.

But none of these held Rambo's interest for long. His roving gaze came to rest on the cabbage lashed to the cabin roof. At twenty inches in diameter, the vegetable was too big to fit through the stern bulkhead.

Rambo stabbed a grubby finger. "Mi laikim dispela kumu." I want this vegetable.

I breathed a private sigh of relief. Losing our primary source of vitamin-C was unfortunate, but less disastrous than say, having to do without a radio or the satellite phone. "April, did you get that?" I bent down so she could hear. "Matey boy here says he wants your cabbage. Best hand it over, eh?"

My new pedalling partner saw the situation rather differently, however. April adored cabbage, especially raw cabbage. Learning of her obsession on Tulagi, Kenny had tracked down the biggest cabbage on the island, an elephantine specimen priced at $120 Solomon Islands dollars, the equivalent of ten pounds sterling. The prize legume would last us almost the entire voyage—a leaf a day enough to keep scurvy at bay.

Until now April had kept herself hidden. Muttering something about her dead body, she thrust her head clear of the hatch and wagged an admonishing finger at Rambo. "Hey, you! Don't even think about it, buddy."

The gunman did a double take. It wasn't every day that pretty blondes materialized out of thin air in the Solomon Islands. He looked like he'd died and gone to *Baywatch* heaven.*

"Get on wit'ya now, ya hear?" April shooed the air like she was waving errant fifth graders back to their classroom. "And keep ya goddamn hands off my cabbage."

Grinning sheepishly, Rambo turned to his friends and shrugged. None of them looked very scary anymore. They were just three naughty

---

* Following the exploits of a posse of scantily clad California lifeguards, the television programme Baywatch enjoys cult status in the South Pacific.

schoolboys being reprimanded for getting carried away playing at soldiers.

"Plees, missus." Rambo held up his hands in mock surrender. "Mitripela nogat laikim bigpela hevi, ookay?" We don't want any problems, okay?

With a sputter of engines, the militiamen bid farewell and off they went, teeth gleaming. I was back on the satellite phone a few seconds later. "Chris, I've got a great story for the evening wire."

July 18, 2000
Wind: ESE 5 knots. Heading: 265M. Position: 09°07'10"S 160°01'19"E
WE STEER A course for the northern tip of Savo Island, its trademark splodge of cloud hovering overhead. "Don't go south of it," the police chief on Tulagi warned. "Militias use Savo to run weapons and food to Guadalcanal." Making a detour this early in the voyage isn't ideal, especially with the trade winds forecast to strengthen over the coming week, but with Cairns over eleven hundred miles away an extra ten won't make that much difference.

The wind is light. A gentle swell rolls in astern. The conditions are perfect for April to start acclimatizing to life on the briny. For now, she looks happy and relaxed—perhaps a little too relaxed.

"It's a lot easier than I thought," she says breezily, pedalling with her hands behind her head. "If I had a pillow back here I could just drift off."

As the afternoon heat index kicks in, we distract ourselves by telling jokes. April starts off with an old favourite: "An Australian and a New Zealander are driving down the road. The Aussie sees a sheep with its head stuck in the fence, so he stops the truck, walks over, and has his way with the sheep."

I've heard this one many times before, usually with an Englishman and a Welshman in place of the Aussie and Kiwi. Nevertheless, it's like hearing the hackneyed gag for the first time coming from the respectable Ms April, dutiful guardian of the young minds of tomorrow.

"When he gets back to the truck, he says to the Kiwi, 'Wow, that was great, you should try it.' So the Kiwi goes over and sticks his head in the fence."

The lavatorial humour segues neatly into a topic that has been weighing heavily on April's mind ever since I wrote her in an email: *Be prepared for the geyser effect when peeing in rough conditions. In other words, seawater shooting up your backside.* At the next shift change, she reaches into one of the compartments and fishes out a white plastic pouch covered in red lettering. "I should probably give this thing a test run now," she says reluctantly, breaking the seal. "Before the waves get any bigger."

I stare at the contents. "Jesus, what *is* that thing?"

Balanced between her fingers is a pink funnel, out of which a short tube extends like a retractable dick.

"I am about to pee off the side of the boat like a man," April announces smugly.

This is all Nancy Sanford's idea. Apparently, she's used these contraptions for years on day trips around Tampa Bay in her Escapade pedal boat.

"Really?" I reply. "With that thing?"

April holds it up for me to inspect. "This nifty device reconfigures the female anatomy from being plumbed on the *inside* to putting the plumbing on the *outside.*"

Explanation complete, April clambers over the side, perches on the emergency oar and positions the plastic penis as per the instructions. "Guaranteed to make a guy jealous," she hollers over her shoulder.

The way I see it, one of the enduring perks of being a man, that sets us apart and makes us feel special and unique in an increasingly metrosexual world, is having a Johnson. Ease of deployment is what it's all about. When you're outdoors and busting for a whiz, whipping out the old trouser snake and letting rip is inestimably superior to scouring the Earth for a bush and then having to wrestle with myriad layers of clothing. Allowing one of our last remaining birthrights to be commandeered by the female species strikes me as just plain wrong.

"You wouldn't have to wait in line for the Ladies bathroom with that thing," I remark disdainfully. "Just go in the Gents, right?"

April nods eagerly. "I reckon. Stand there with the fellas, talking about football, drinking beer—"

"And how you couldn't get it up last night because your strap-on got jammed."

April blushes and falls silent. Rocking to the rhythm of the swell, she holds onto the sliding hatch with one hand and her gender bender gizmo with the other. A full minute goes by. Nothing happens.

"Taking your own sweet time, aren't you, Ms A?"

"I can't go here," she wails. "There's too much water. I can't pee with this much water."

"Of course there's too much water. It's the Pacific Ocean."

"No, I mean too much water sloshing up around my knees."

Every time *Moksha* heels to starboard, seawater spills over the gunwales, soaking April to the waist.

"Stop procrastinating."

"But the boat's rocking too wildly. I might drop it."

We can only hope, I mutter to myself. "For goodness' sake!" I yell. "I've never seen such a bloody performance."

"I'm trying."

"If you spent this long pedalling, we'd be in Cairns by now."

"You try this, then. You try it. You try to hang something off between your legs and pee."

"That's what I do five times a day, sweetheart."

A freak wave suddenly appears, tipping *Moksha* to port and sending

April sprawling into the cockpit. The funnel slips from her fingers and disappears into the drink.

"What the hell are you doing, April?" The opportunity to poke fun is too good to pass up. "You're supposed to be having a pee not practicing for the summer Olympics."

April is hanging monkey-like between the oars, groping for handholds. Incapacitated by giggles, she sinks into the bilges and babbles something unintelligible.

"What was that?"

"I just peed all over myself."

"Oh dear. Are you sure you read the instructions properly?"

Reaching for the empty packet, April reads aloud: "Easy to use off sides of boats!"

July 19

Wind: SE 25 knots. Heading: 210M. Position: 09°09'47"S 159°35'28"E

SKIRTING THE WESTERNMOST point of Guadalcanal, Coral Sea Corner as we later call it, the wind accelerates to thirty knots and all hell breaks loose. No longer in the protective lee of land, we are now exposed to the full power of the Southeast Trades sweeping unchallenged across the Pacific from South America. The seas around us become steep and confused, upshot of the confluence of winds, tides, and currents ricocheting between the islands. For every mile we pedal south, we lose six west.

Then it starts to rain. Heavily.

I awake at first light on the second day to a hollow clanking sound. Our camp kettle is floating in six inches of water and bouncing between the plywood storage bins. A half eaten bowl of waterlogged porridge is on the move, along with my sandals. Outside, the wind shrieks. April has been pedalling since 3:00 am, steering in total darkness, wrestling the toggles back and forth to keep *Moksha* from broaching and capsizing. Sceptics denounced as reckless and irresponsible my intention to invite a woman aboard without any nautical experience. Yet here she is, handling the boat no problem. Fortunately, she's taken the trouble to get fit before coming out. An expedition first!

Her exuberance is gone, though. So, too, the carefree tone in her voice as she gives a rundown of the second graveyard shift: "Started to feel queasy about five o'clock." She takes a swig of green isotonic drink from her water bottle. "Also, I think I've worked out what my biggest fear is."

"What's that?"

"Not feeling a hundred per cent, and not being able to give a hundred per cent."

I corral my sandals and begin bailing with the stray porridge bowl. It's hardly worth the effort. As fast as it goes out, the water comes back in as rain or crashing waves. It's more for my sanity. I know from past voyages how the sound of water slopping in the bilges will begin to grate on my nerves after a while.

Getting to Cairns was never going to be easy. The Coral Sea has a long-standing reputation with mariners for being one of the most violent, unpredictable bodies of water in the world. In the early planning stages, while poring over pilot charts of the South Pacific, my attention was immediately drawn to the little wind rose icons. For July and August they displayed four, sometimes five flags set at four o'clock—force 4 to 5 from the southeast. In and of itself, this is no big deal. *Moksha* can cope with much stronger winds, up to gale force 10. The problem is gaining 500 miles of southing to reach Cairns, the nearest port of entry on the Australian mainland.* Making headway against such winds looks to be a far greater challenge than I first anticipated.

The alternative was to aim for the port of entry on Thursday Is-

---

* As a prerequisite for entering any country with water as a border, recognized ports of entry are equipped to clear foreign vessels through customs, quarantine, and immigration. In the case of Australia, making landfall in an unauthorized port can incur thousands of dollars' worth of penalties.

land in the Torres Straits, the narrow neck of water separating Cape York from Papua New Guinea. But with twelve-knot tidal streams and a minefield of reefs to negotiate, the risk of being blown off course and wrecked is too great.

So Cairns it is. Even so, watching the waves slam one after the other against *Moksha's* port beam, sending torrents cascading through the hatch, a gnawing doubt takes shape in my mind: *What if we can't make Cairns?*

Everything is against us. The wind is blowing us northwest. The waves are pushing us northwest. Most worrying of all, a one-and-a-half-knot current is taking us northwest.* The entire Pacific appears to be in cahoots, intent on ejecting us out of its watery domain and onto the reef systems east of Papua New Guinea. Even if we manage to miss these, the serrated jaws of the world's largest living structure, the Great Barrier Reef, stretching some 1,600 miles along the Queensland coast, lie in wait a further 500 miles to the west.

To avert disaster, we need to pedal one mile south for every two we lose west, making it imperative to keep *Moksha's* bow pointing south at all times. R&R is a luxury we can't afford. Even spending time to enjoy a meal is out of the question. For every minute the cranks don't turn, *Moksha* drifts fifty yards closer to the reefs. There is no cushion. No margin for error. Without a motor or a sail, we have only one option.

Keep pedalling.

July 22
Wind: SE 15-20 knots. Heading: 180M. Position: 09°47'46"S 158°11'40"E
TORRENTIAL RAIN ALL morning. The inside of the central compartment resembles a Chinese laundry with sodden bras, knickers, and towels swinging from the emergency oars. In the last 24 hours, we've made

---

* A force of nature immune to *Moksha's* streamlined shape above and below the waterline.

eleven miles south to thirty-three west, a ratio of one to three. This isn't good enough. Our course over ground now has us on a collision course with the easternmost reef of the Louisiades Archipelago, Pocklington Reef.

April's seasickness has also worsened. On Tulagi, I'd confidently informed her that it would take only a day or two to acclimatize. "Three tops, then you'll be a hundred per cent." I was wrong.

Quivering flashes light up the southern horizon as night draws in. With every stuttering discharge, the darkening sea glistens like a lake of crude oil. It's my turn to take the first stint in the Rathole. I wake to a yelp and thunderclaps booming all around. The nightlight on my watch reads 00:56. *Time to relieve April.*

My crewmate looks wide-eyed in the beam of my headlamp, not a trace of tiredness in her chalky face. Not many things unnerve April, but lightning is clearly one of them. "It's been one wild, wild night," she whispers. "Rain. Lightning. Wind blowing like crazy. Horizontal sheets of water. It's been really, really black."

She leans forward and squints at the red compass light. "And all I've seen is that 180 to 210 degrees. Seems like I've been going around in a big circle all night."

Removing the wooden chock and shifting the pedal seat back for my longer legs, she peels away her sweat-drenched towel and we make the switch, shuffling past each other in the darkness. I grab the steering toggles and turn *Moksha's* bow to 180 degrees. April makes a beeline for the still warm sleeping bag.

July 25
Wind: ESE 10 knots. Heading: 180M. Position: 11°04'36"S 156°00'46"E
HOORAH! A LULL in the trades has allowed us to claw twenty-five miles south, enough to scrape past Pocklington Reef. If we can next avoid Rossel and Tagula Islands, we'll have a straight shot to Australia.

I film April as I pedal. She's sitting on the passenger seat, wedged across the inside of the cabin, writing her first email.

"Success?" I ask.

"Success." She sighs heavily, closes the laptop lid and removes her purple-rimmed glasses. "But now I'm going to have to lie down for just a quick minute."

"Feeling queasy?"

She nods and pries off a sodden white sock. "Looking down seems to be my Achilles heel." The soles of her feet are starting to rot, the skin turning white and flaky like spoiled cheddar cheese. Painful lesions mark the straps of her ill-fitting sandals—the reason for the socks.

"Just tell yourself, 'I'm not going to throw up. I'm not going to throw up'."

This is easier said than done. Seasickness is one of the most debilitating conditions known to mankind, the marine equivalent of mad cow disease, lobotomizing its victims and reducing them to the competency of a day-old baby.

April makes a face. "God, will it ever, ever get better?"

"It will."

"I'm really tired of throwing up, though."

"I know. Keep in there. You'll be a salty sea bitch by the end of this, gobbling vindaloos for breakfast with a force ten blowing."

Hand held to her forehead, she looks despairingly out over the lumpy blue. "You think?"

"Absolutely."

Privately, however, I'm beginning to wonder. We've been at sea a week. If anything her seasickness is getting worse.

"Okay," she whispers. "It's just taking longer than I thought." She works her way feet first into the Rathole, expels another deep sigh, and lowers her head onto a rolled-up fleece jacket that serves as a communal pillow. With her eyes closed and arms crossed over her chest, I can't help thinking of a corpse ready for burial at sea.

After an hour of sleep, April rallies. Determined to pull her own weight, she insists on cooking the evening meal while I pedal. Balancing the breadboard on her knees, she tries to peel an onion, riding the waves as she would a bronco back in Colorado. Before long her eyes glaze and her face turns white. She reels like a drunk, exhaling noisily. Setting the board down and scrambling to her feet, she begins retching violently over the side. Only bile comes up. All she's been able to hold down the last 24 hours is a little water.

"It's like morning sickness, only worse," she groans, slumping back to the passenger seat and covering her face with her hands.

To make matters worse, she's been having lucid nightmares, a side effect of the anti-malarials we still have to take after our time in the mosquito-ridden Solomons.

"Last night it was a roller coaster. The car I was in climbed higher and higher. We took off and that first swoop in the stomach was terrifying. So real, like it was actually happening! Then I noticed my daughter, Lacey, standing below the tracks. She was just a toddler, her little arms reaching up to me. Except that her hands were gone, sliced at the wrists …"

She halts part way through the sentence, the imagery too disturbing. Eventually, she recovers enough composure to continue. "I've had other dreams where I've felt threatened or overwhelmed by an aura of tremendous evil, the pit of my stomach filled with impending doom."

The wind strengthens during the night. By morning, cresting waves are once again pounding our port beam, the boat shuddering with every blow. In spite of this, April is determined to carry out something she's been looking forward to since day one.

Washing her hair.

"I can't arrive in Cairns with high seas hair, now can I?"

"Why not?" I counter. "Better high seas hair than Barbie hair. No one will ever believe you've just pedalled a thousand miles through some of the roughest water in the world if you step off the boat wearing hair curlers."

My objection, unsurprisingly, is overruled. Gathering umpteen bottles and a flask of vinegar for untangling knots, April edges to the stern and secures the paraphernalia with bungee cords before any of it rolls overboard. She hugs the rear compartment with her thighs to maintain balance and begins dousing her hair with seawater using a plastic tea mug. *Moksha* bucks and heaves, and hissing waves collapse unnervingly close.

Wet hair flailing in the wind, April massages a dollop of shampoo into her scalp. A wall of water suddenly explodes, engulfing the stern. My crewmate reappears several seconds later, hanging onto the safety line for dear life.

"This is a pain!" she gasps, eyes screwed shut from the stinging shampoo. "A real pain in the ass!"

Having a woman aboard, I'm starting to realize, is a double-edged sword. On the one hand, there isn't the same clash of egos you get with two men. No sucking of teeth and *"Ooh, you don't want to do it like that, mate"* every time something needs fixing. Women are also easier on the eye and stronger psychologically. "My ambition is to be like the Energizer Bunny," April had told me after refusing to relinquish her 3:00 am graveyard shift, "known for going and going." Woozy with seasickness and without a murmur of complaint, she'd clambered out of the warm cocoon of the Rathole into the freezing cockpit, wriggled into her waterlogged socks, and got to work.

On the flip side, April's long, blonde hair has become an integral part of on-board life. Hairballs lurk in the porridge. Loose strands work their way around the cranks. Even the little twelve-volt cooling fan becomes clogged and has to be dismantled every few days. The novelty of being smacked in the face repeatedly by a barrage of soggy underwear whilst pedalling is also wearing thin.

Smirking, I stand in the open hatch and watch April do battle with her arsenal of bottles, combs, hairbrushes, and razors. She's soaked and bedraggled, her hair plastered to her scalp like a drowned cat. Keeping a firm hold of the safety line, she uses her free hand to try to release a tangle.

"Just like taking a shower back home, eh, Ms A?" I pick up the camcorder and press record.

"Oh, just like," she replies testily. "Just like."

"Anything I can do to help?"

"Take that camera away so I can rinse off."

"I'm not stopping you."

She looks at me witheringly. "I've got nothing on underneath, and I'm freezing. I just wanna rinse off and get dry."

"Alright, alright, keep your knickers on—or rather off. Ha!"

"Yeah, well, a person can't always be Mary flippin' Sunshine. And just remember, your short and curlies are within my reach."

Back in the central compartment, I enquire as to whether the whole exercise has been worth it. April's teeth are chattering. Her shoulders are stooped with cold. She clings with grim determination to the port side oar like it's the last life raft off the *Titanic*.

"Most definitely. It was a wonderful experience."

"Really?"

She glances away. "Well … actually … no. It wasn't a wonderful experience. It was an *awful* experience. But it feels good to be clean." A lone seabird skims effortlessly over the white caps, using the deftest of wing movements. "Mentally, I'm finding it's worth keeping a few routines from land," she adds wistfully, tracking the bird. "It's the little things that make all the difference out here, that help you stay human."

I'd come to the same conclusion on the Atlantic and adopted pet projects I called Created Value tasks to trigger involvement and sustain interest, making life aboard more bearable.

"I still preferred your hair encrusted with salt," I say jokingly. "Complemented the swashbuckling look. Rather suited you."

"At least I have hair, Mister Lewis. You're going bald."

Touché.

"Talking of which," I reply, reaching inside the starboard side netting, "I thought of a way to keep your hair from getting matted in future." The blue-handled scissors are pockmarked with corrosion and streaked with rust, the edges blunt as hell. Ever since my brass dividers went missing on Tulagi, I've been using them to plot our daily position. They've been used for a variety of other tasks, too, everything from scraping barnacles to cutting rotten carrots to pruning toenails.

"Come to Freddy." I snap the blades. "Snip, snip."

April looks horrified. "Get away from me with that thing!"

The wind slackens late afternoon, the rain peters out, and for a few delightful hours before sunset the Coral Sea draws breath and turns its malicious eye elsewhere. April emerges reborn after two hours in the Rathole. She sits on the passenger seat, her hair straight and free of knots, looking lovely in her green lava-lava. Her efforts, I have to admit, have been worthwhile. She stares out across the undulating rollers, and for the first time since Coral Sea Corner, the nearest thing to serenity steals across her face.

"Don't worry, Mister Lewis," she says softly. "I'll look every bit the pirate princess when I step off this boat in Australia."

I stop pedalling for a moment to slip Van Morrison's *Moondance* into the CD player. The sun sinks smouldering into the sea as the Belfast man's nasal whine fills the cabin, punctuated by staccato stabs of brass.

We were born before the wind

Also younger than the sun

Ere the bonnie boat was won

As we sailed into the mystic

April taps out a rhythm on the same oar she was clinging to earlier. Funny, I think to myself, how music can change one's perspective so quickly. One minute you're cursing your gypsy soul for getting you into such a cluster fuck in the first place. Next, you're celebrating how fortunate you are to be experiencing a truly magical domain few will ever get to see.

Hark, now hear the sailors cry
Smell the sea and feel the sky
Let your soul and spirit fly into the mystic …

I download email the following morning. My parent's neighbour has just been diagnosed with pancreatic cancer. Richard is otherwise healthy, in his early forties, energetic, funny, intelligent, with a loving wife and now only three weeks to live. Without any warning, it's all over.

At the core of life, I'm reminded, is transience. The good times, the bad times, they're all illusions. Especially the bad times. "This too shall pass," as the saying goes. The only thing we can really count on is that nothing stays the same.

July 28
Wind: SSE 25 knots. Heading: 180M. Position: 11°47'27"S 154°26'12"E
I STARE INCREDULOUSLY at the two-tone screen of the GPS. In the past 24 hours, we've lost forty-two miles west and gained only a handful south. Disaster looms once again. To avoid running aground on the reef east of Tagula, we need to make fifteen miles south over the next fifteen hours. The likelihood of this happening is slim given the recent trend.

All we can do differently is try to increase our RPMs. April ups hers from forty to forty-five. I aim for fifty-two. To further optimize performance, we shorten the daytime shifts from three to two hours and the night-time ones from four to three.

"It's like pushing a loaded wagon up a hill," April remarks, her knees visibly straining.

"It's going to take a full-on effort," I agree.

"Better cowboy up, then!"

Good old April.

I power up the GPS at the next shift change. April waits patiently to hear whether she's made the all-important one-mile-south-per-hour ratio.

"So what happens if I don't meet my quota?" she asks.

While the GPS is looking for satellites, I fold my sweat towel into thirds, arrange it against the back of the pedal seat, and get cranking. "Then I'm afraid you'll leave me no choice."

Her face falls. "No choice?"

"But to get out the cat."

"The cat? What cat?"

"Cat o'nine tails."

"Ooh! Promise?"

Not exactly the response I was expecting. "Tell you what, Ms April. If we miss this bloody reef, we'll celebrate with an extra special treat, okay?"

Fifteen hours later

I READ OFF the latest coordinates and pencil them onto the Admiralty chart draped over my knees, as I've done every half an hour since our cat o'nine tails banter. The top half of the chart is now covered with hastily scribbled letters and figures—date-time groups, latitude and longitude positions, arithmetic calculations—chronicling our frantic bid to make ground south.

April stops pedalling to hear the final verdict. It's the first time in fifteen hours the cranks have been at rest longer than the sixty-odd seconds it takes to switch positions.

Wobbling my pencil between thumb and forefinger, I smile at my exhausted co-pedaller. "I have some excellent news to report, April.

In the last fifteen hours we've made eighteen miles south, five of them during your last shift."

She beams with pleasure.

"Well done." I rap the pencil triumphantly on the chart. "Extra tot of rum for the crew tonight, bosun!"

Missing Tagula Reef is huge, putting us back in the running to reach Cairns. I duly extend to April the honour of being the first to sample The Cabbage, which we've been saving as long as possible. She unlashes it from the cabin roof and peels away the spoiled, outer leaves, revealing a pristine inner membrane that glistens with the polished luminosity of a living brain.

"Jeepers!" she gasps, turning the vegetable slowly between her fingers like it was an ancient treasure. "Just look at the size of it. Beautiful, isn't it?" Her eyes close in ecstasy as she tears off a leaf and takes a bite. "This is pure self-indulgence. Forgive me, but I love cabbage. Loved it ever since I was a child." She takes another bite, the greenery snapping like toast. "Absolutely the best cabbage I've ever tasted … been dreaming about it for ages …" She's rambling now, delirious with pleasure. "So expensive … but so good …"

August 2

Wind: SSE 30 knots. Heading: 210M. Position: 12°57'17"S 153°19'25"E

THE MORNING OF the fifteenth day breaks cold and dreary with relentless rain, the ocean windswept. An eerie blue light penetrates the cabin, at the end of which a silhouetted form sways in the half-light. Eyes closed, fist propping up her chin, April dozes as she pedals. Her green lava-lava tied across the stern window is ready to catch her head when it falls.

The wind has veered south-southeast in the night and freshened to thirty knots with forty-knot gusts. The best we can now manage is 210 degrees magnetic, taking us diagonally over the backs of the sweeping rollers, some of which shape-shift into spitting balls of liquid rage and target the cockpit with laser-like precision. We're back to being constantly wet and longing for the sun. *The voyage is becoming a dodgem ride in the Twilight Zone*, I scribble in my journal, *complete with buckets of water being dumped over our heads at regular intervals.*

Normally, I prefer the livelier conditions, far preferable to a dull, millpond existence with the sun beating down. But with everything soaked and no foreseeable prospect of any of it drying out, the ocean is wearing us down twice as fast.

Our 24-hour fix is predictably disastrous. As well as the by now familiar double-digit west, we've been driven two miles north. North! Going backwards dredges up memories of the dreaded countercurrent between Hawaii and Tarawa. Deploying the sea anchor would be pointless. To win back the lost ground, we'll have to do it the hard way. I'm just hoping beyond hope this is only a temporary weather anomaly and not the seasonal norm.

"I don't know what day it is," April suddenly blurts out, giving voice to an air of disillusionment that has crept into the voyage. "I don't know the date. I don't even know the time." She laughs the hollow laugh of someone who is beyond caring. "I just know this ocean continues to move in the wrong direction for me."

Increasingly, especially during my graveyard shifts, I catch myself turning my ocean ring like a devotional prayer wheel, contemplating the mercurial temperament of the she-ocean I married. Things started out well between us after tying the knot outside the Golden Gate Bridge, the crossing to Hawaii as idyllic and harmonious as any honeymooning couple could have hoped for. A slight misunderstanding surfaced in the doldrums mid-Pacific, but by the Solomon Islands our relationship was back on track. On this voyage, in particular, I've taken great care to remain attentive to her moods in the hope of pre-empting any furious outbursts. Yet, for all the pampering, my thalassic bride appears wholly bent on our destruction, capable of only the briefest glimpses of matrimonial charity.

I wonder. Perhaps she takes exception to having a woman on board?

August 5
Wind: SE 15-20 knots. Heading: 170M. Position: 12°57'22"S 152°04'54"E
"WHAT'VE YOU EATEN in the last twenty-four hours, Ms A?"

Her eyes sunken and glazed and besieged by dark rings, April nurses a handful of raw oats. She sorts between thumb and forefinger and places a few loose grains in her mouth. The bones in her face protrude as she chews.

"A Cliff Bar," she replies faintly. "A *GU* energy sachet, and a tangerine."

I shake my head. "Abso-lutely-useless. That's not enough to sustain a fly."

"It sustained me during my last shift," she retorts, snatching at a steering toggle to correct *Moksha's* heading.

"Maybe, but you're losing too much weight. Soon we'll be measuring your pedal rotations in RPC, not RPM."

My partner stares at me nonplussed.

"Revolutions per century?"

It's an underhand comment, especially in light of her unremitting seasickness, but it's one of the few ways I can get her to eat. Becoming a burden to the voyage is still her biggest fear.

I spoon a single dollop of cooked porridge onto a tin plate and hand it to her.

"I can't eat anymore," she moans. "I tried."

As well as stubbornness—ironically, one of the qualities I chose her for in the first place—things aren't helped by April's deep-seated hostil-

ity towards porridge. The Breakfast of Champions for the Scots trans-
lates to the Breakfast of Privation for Americans, the generally reviled
oatmeal, synonymous with the hardships and austerities endured by
their gruel-eating forebears in feudal Europe. Unfortunately, this can't
be helped. Following the Great Weevil Infestation of the last voyage,
when all the pancake mix had to be chucked overboard, porridge is the
only breakfast option we have.

I push the bowl at her. "C'mon, Ms A. Gotta keep those legs turning. Doesn't taste that bad, surely?"

She contemplates the glob with barely concealed revulsion. "Hmm,
looks delightful. And so much of it."

"What do you mean so much of it? There's hardly anything there!"

"How about half now, half later?"

"I don't think so. We had an arrangement, remember?"

The evening before we'd received an email from John Castanha,
April's fellow teacher and personal trainer in Colorado. Having read
the daily blogs, he, too, is concerned for her health.

April, he wrote, *if it hasn't already, your body will start consuming its own
muscles for fuel - unless you eat.*

Best of luck, Coach John

*PS. How many times a day do you vomit? Your fifth graders are looking forward
to watching it on video.*

Presented with an opinion she trusts in matters of sports nutrition,
April agreed to a deal. For every three square meals she manages to
choke down, I will desalinate an extra litre of fresh water to put towards
her hair washing.

"The porridge is getting cold, April. Do you want to wash your hair
or not?"

"Yes, of course."

I hand her a spoon. "Well then. Eat, woman. If nothing else, eat for
your country!"

She prods the now-congealed lump as if it might come to life. Reluctantly, she takes a tiny bite.

"You eat like a sparrow," I scoff.

She puts the spoon down—glad of the excuse. "Well, I've never seen anyone consume food as fast as you do. You just woof it, woof it!"

Another email, this one from my father, has re-floated the idea of trying to reach Thursday Island instead of Cairns. As he points out, we have to make significant progress south, and soon, or face being wrecked somewhere along the 500-mile stretch of Barrier Reef north of Cooktown. Thursday Island is currently downwind of our position. We could be there in a week, complete customs and immigration formalities, and then continue down the west coast of Cape York to the mining town of Weipa. After making official landfall and the all-important media splash, April could be back in Colorado before school starts, leaving me to get stuck into fundraising for the next leg.

Oh, that it were so simple. There is the small matter of navigating without charts through the complex reef systems of the Torres Straits. Captain William Bligh managed it in a twenty-three-foot open dory after being set adrift by the *Bounty* mutineers in 1789, but he had the luxury of canvas to prevail against the powerful winds and currents.

One possible solution is for Our Man Brown to drop the requisite charts from a light aircraft, like he did the cheese, beer, and oranges in the Caribbean. Another is for my father to plot a passage through the reefs and email us the latitude and longitude coordinates to plug into our GPS. Either way, the thought of bouncing like a pinball through the Torres Straits doesn't fill me with a huge amount of confidence. Just a few hundred yards off course, not inconceivable given our limited horsepower, and we'd be finished.

"Let's give it another twenty-four hours," I suggest to April after we've discussed both options. "Decide between Cairns and Thursday Island after our next position fix."

That evening, I fire up the laptop to type the lesson plan that April has prepared in her head. She dictates as she pedals, too sick to look at the screen herself. Three or more hours of each day is currently dedicated to educational outreach: updating the blog, writing lesson extensions for schools, editing photos, a video clip, then uploading it all through the tortuously slow satellite modem. Today's mathematics lesson examines how many times April pukes in a 24-hour period.

Being kids, they'll love it.

August 6
Wind: SE 10 knots. Heading: 180M. Position: 13°01'55"S 152°02'55"E
A RAY OF hope. We've made seven miles south in the last 24 hours, the first net gain in nearly three days. It's enough to keep the Cairns option alive—for the time being, at least.

"That's *such* good news!" April exclaims happily.

Optimism rekindled, I go over the side to scrape barnacles while April pedals. Doing this while the boat is underway, hanging onto a gunwale with one hand and working vigorously with the other, would normally be a no-no; the memory of nearly drowning mid-Atlantic after being separated from the boat still haunts me. But in view of our most recent GPS reading, I decide the risk is worth it. Any reduction in drag will help leverage the southerly trend and win us ground towards Cairns.

August 9
Wind: ESE 10 knots. Heading: 170M. Position: 13°05'28"S 150°15'29"E
THIS IS BIZARRE. Here we are flying south on the same ocean that was pushing us north only a few days ago. In the last three hours alone, we've gained eight miles south and lost only five west.

"Do you think Thursday Island is definitely out of the picture?" asks April, huddling into her jacket on the passenger seat. It's getting colder the further south we go. For the first time since leaving San Francisco, extra layers are needed mornings and evenings.

I'm cautiously optimistic about reaching Cairns, but I don't want to get our hopes up just yet. "Too early to tell," I reply. "Ultimately, the ocean will decide for us. All we can do in the meantime is pedal."

In a yacht or a motorboat, we wouldn't be obsessing over every mile. We'd simply raise more canvas or open the throttle. Self-determination in a human-powered craft is a less exact science, however, especially when crossing a body of water as capricious as the Coral Sea. To ward off the inevitable uncertainty and disappointment, we strive to supress expectations, treating good and bad progress with equal indifference.

A rare display of Coral Sea life interrupts the drudgery. A pair of dark, torpedo shapes begin circling the boat—Risso's dolphins according to the quick reference card. They're both over ten feet long with blunt snouts, a feature that sets them apart from their cuddly bottlenose cousins. The Risso's are also streaked with white lacerations, battle scars from the deep-water squid on which they feed.

April stands in the hatchway watching the animals huff and puff through their blowholes, a show of aggression to frighten off the strange yellow creature that has blundered into their realm.

"Ooh, look!" April points in excitement. "Here they come."

The Risso's accelerate in attack formation, surfing in the face of an incoming wave. They look certain to ram us, re-enacting the final moments before Captain Ahab's terrible reckoning. At the last possible second, they break left and right, disappearing with a great flourish of tails.

August 10

Wind: SE 10 knots. Heading: 170M. Position: 13°25'26"S 149°41'43"E

CAIRNS IS 240 nautical miles away. So close, and yet so far! If we can pedal one mile south every hour, we could be there in ten days. The question is how long we can keep up this punishing regime. We're walking a fine line between keeping the good ship moving forward and being too tired to operate her safely. To maintain RPMs, we reduce the daytime shifts from two hours to one and a half.

It's been three weeks since we left Tulagi. April continues to be seasick. She looks anorexic, her body covered in bruises, one of several indicators that starvation is taking hold. Her feet are also swollen. Her eyelids droop. She wears a deadpan, thousand-yard stare that bores into the blues and whites comprising our watery universe. She's doing her best to eat three meals a day, but I don't push it anymore. A few mouthfuls of food and she blows it out in chunks. Painful saltwater sores are appearing on the backs of her arms and legs.

Even more alarmingly, she's haemorrhaging blood: dysfunctional uterine bleeding, according to her GP in Colorado who we managed to reach via the satellite phone. It's another symptom of severe malnourishment, apparently, a by-product of the hormones getting knocked out of whack. In a drastic attempt at self-preservation, her body is slowly digesting itself from the inside out.

Not that April seems to notice. She still refuses to let me pedal any of her shifts. My admiration for her resilience in the face of so much hardship is matched only by a growing sense of guilt at her chronic seasickness.

"After all my talk of scoffing vindaloos for breakfast with a force ten blowing," I remark sheepishly.

"But you know what," April replies, "I wouldn't trade this for the world. This is my new greatest adventure."

Our southerly advance has slowed, and we're starting to slip west again. With the Great Barrier Reef closing in, there'll come a point in the next week when we simply run out of ocean. Thursday Island is no longer an option. When I tell April we need to "pull out all the stops and give it one last push to Cairns," she doesn't even blink.

August 11

Wind: SE 15-20 knots. Heading: 170M. Position: 13°57'51"S 148°52'12"E

"WHAT ARE YOU looking forward to right now, April?"

I peer at her through the camcorder lens. Wet towels, tee shirts, and flapping underwear form a narrow corridor at the end of which she perches on the pedal seat.

"A baked p'tata with sour cream—lots and lots of sour cream—and a big green salad, with t'mata. And blue cheese dressing."

"You mean a po-ta-to and to-ma-to?" I tease, stressing the British pronunciation.

"U-huh. Boy, wouldn't that be good." Closing her eyes, April stretches out her hand as though reaching for a mirage. "I can see it, almost taste it."

"You better get pedalling, then, 'cos all we've got left are two onions, some rancid garlic, and the remains of The Cabbage, which is starting to look a bit nasty."

For the last 48 hours, April has bled continuously, depleting her of life-sustaining fluids and increasing the risk of isotonic dehydration. She's also run out of sanitary pads. With no other clean, absorbent material available, she's resorted to cutting up the sweat-encrusted towels we use to line the pedal seat, adding infection as a possible complication. The only good news is a temporary lull in her seasickness accompanied by a renewed interest in food. I jump at the opportunity to get some down her. Taking stock of the available ingredients, I give the meal options.

"It's either curry, curry, or curry. So what's it going to be?"

"Curry sounds good."

"Excellent choice."

Together with the last of the veggies, I use two cans of tomatoes, one can of kidney beans, and a few sticks of bean curd. I add walnuts, raisins, dried apricots, pepper, one cup of seawater, and a dash of curry powder for taste but not enough to aggravate her stomach. The result is a big communal stockpot, a refuelling bowser we can dip into whenever we need energy.

I take the first graveyard shift. Around midnight, I feel the pedal system tighten. The propeller shaft shears a moment later, and the cranks spin free.

This is the first time a pedal unit has failed at night. It's bad enough trying to fix one in daylight with heavy seas pummelling the boat. In darkness, and with the wind gusting forty knots, it'll be a nightmare. Lying beam-on to the waves, *Moksha* starts to corkscrew, and waves crash through the open hatch. A shaft of feeble yellow light from my headlamp provides the nearest thing to illumination.

Trying not to wake April, I lift the unit free of the stainless box, remove The Dog's Bollocks collar, and set about detaching the grease cap from the bottom bracket using a pair of Channellock pliers. It's well and truly jammed, welded by corrosion. Frustrated, I give it a good yank. The thing comes away with a great sucking PLOP! followed by a deluge of emulsified grease spewing into my lap.

Then the headlamp dims, flickers, and dies completely.

I just sit there for a minute, mute with disbelief. The puddle of oil slides into my crotch before joining the pool of water sloshing around my ankles. The lubricant quickly spreads, forming a mini slick that slurps and gurgles wickedly in the darkness. A flashback to the Atlantic reminds me of what to expect for the remainder of the voyage. Grease will become our constant companion, finding its way into our food, hair, ears, clothes, and sleeping bag.

Spare headlamp batteries are in the sleeping compartment. Half-way across the cabin, I lose my footing and nearly pitch head first into the Rathole with April. She wakes to a catalogue of hissing profanity.

"Is there anything you need help with?" she murmurs groggily.

As it happens, there is. I need a decent light to do the repair, and the brightest one we have is the halogen lamp on the camcorder. A minute later, April is sitting gingerly on the passenger seat (she has sores on her backside now), holding the camera as steady as conditions will allow.

"Might as well roll tape while you're at it," I tell her.

The propeller has to be separated from the broken shaft and then fitted to one of the replacement pedal units from the stern compartment. *Moksha* continues to wallow, and water crashes over the side. With no spare hands for bailing, the slick rises to our knees.

"It's like trying to fix a lawnmower in your living room," I explain to the camera. "Except the place is flooded, the walls and the furniture are all covered in motor oil, and the room's going round and round like a fairground ride on steroids."

April stares intently at the LCD screen, keeping the beam of light trained on my filthy fingers. Occasionally, she has to whip the camera under her jacket to shield it from an incoming wave. Ten minutes pass. The camera light dies. I describe to April the whereabouts of a fresh battery inside the Rathole and how to load it on the back of the camera. Eventually, we resume, now soaked to the skin and plastered in grease.

The propeller shows no interest in budging. A hammer would be nice, but it's lying on the seabed somewhere between Hawaii and Tarawa. The only stout object to hand is the breadboard. A few seconds of heavy pounding and the shaft finally gives, dislodging a vital nut that skitters off the sacrificial brass peg and disappears into the oily muck.

"Fuuucckk!"

April has held out as long as she can. She turns white, hands me the camera, and makes a lunge for the side. A sweeping arc of vomit follows, splattering into the slick, adding curry to the oleaginous concoction. Remembering our promise to Kenny to film everything, I keep the camera running, capturing what is by now a well-rehearsed performance of feeding the fishes.

"I'm sorry," April gasps between retches. "So sorry."

Stomach empty once more, she sinks back to the passenger seat.

"April," I say, cringing. "I have one last request, I'm afraid. Stupidly, I had the microphone turned off. Do you think you could do that last bit again? Just go through the motions so Kenny has some audio to work with. The whole sequence will be useless otherwise."

As always, it's the shit-hitting-the-fan episodes that make for the most engaging footage, one of the more perverse realities of documentary filmmaking.

April smiles thinly. "Sure."

"Just for a few seconds. Thanks, you're a real sport."

She leans obligingly over the side and pretends to dry retch. The sound is pitiful. She even groans for effect.

"Great performance!" I say once she's back inside. "Especially the groaning. Very convincing."

"Actually," she whispers, "I didn't have to act. There can't be that many people who can barf on demand. I must have a special talent, huh?"

I pass her the camera so I can finish putting the unit back together, hammering the collar in place with the breadboard and securing the crank arms with a hex key. Changeover complete, I slide the replacement unit down through the stainless box, guiding the propeller by hand.

We've been dead in the water for nearly two and a half hours, taking us five miles closer to the Barrier Reef. It's time to get going.

I look at April. She's shivering and horribly seasick. Again.

"Okay, get thee to bed woman."

"Let me help clean up."

"No, get your arse in the Rathole."

"I guess that's a wrap, then," she mutters, before crawling into the sleeping bag.

August 14

Wind: SE 30-35 knots. Heading: 165M. Position: 14°34'03"S 145°54'26"E
ANOTHER HELLISH NIGHT. First, the GPS packed up. Then the trades strengthened to thirty-five knots, barring us from making any further ground south. *The Coral Sea is not only a cruel sea*, I scrawl in my increasingly soggy journal. *It is a vindictive one. We seem to be living out some Sisyphean ordeal here: a ray of hope offered, then snatched away.*

With the Great Barrier Reef a mere fifteen miles off our starboard beam, reaching Cairns, 150 miles still to the south, is now all but impossible. We face the one scenario I was trying at all costs to avoid. The northeast coast of Cape York has no safe harbour and no rescue service. Running aground on the reef will almost certainly mean losing *Moksha* and possibly our own lives. As it is, April continues to haemorrhage blood for the sixth day in a row. She is in desperate need of medical treatment.

Examining the charts, I notice an island due west of our position, eleven miles inside the armour of the outer reef. Lizard Island is home to a research station and five-star holiday resort, according to the cruising guide. One or other is bound to have a doctor. If not, an airstrip is marked. *Moksha* could be moored in the lee; April could be medevaced to a hospital in Cairns; I would have time to figure out what to do next.

The only problem is getting there.

Blocking our path is a line of ribbon reefs, impenetrable barricades of coral stretching up to twenty miles before an opening. Such gaps when they do occur are tiny, some less than a hundred yards across. Navigating *Moksha* through one of these will be like posting a paper airplane through a letterbox on the opposite side of the street.

Nevertheless, it is our best hope.

I draw up a plan to bisect the reef at Cormorant Pass, a 200-yard keyhole east of Lizard. Timing will be critical. We have to be outside the entrance exactly one hour after low water to catch the tide flowing in the right direction: from east to west. The tide tables show only one feasible window every 24 hours. Miss it, and we'll be wrecked on Yonge Reef to the northwest.

The best opportunity looks to be this Thursday, August 17, at 4:37 pm. That's seventy-two hours from now. There'll still be daylight, and the moon is on the wane, offering a more subdued tide. The trouble is our drift. Even pedalling south-southeast, directly into the wind and current, we're losing two miles west every hour. This will put us outside the entrance in less than fifteen hours.

We need more time.

I deploy the sea anchor, a parachute device made of lightweight canvas that acts as a drag through the water. Our speed drops to less than one knot, a notable improvement, but there's a price. Lying stern to the waves, *Moksha* rolls violently as if rubbed between two giant hands. April's nausea worsens, and for the first time since leaving Tulagi, I, too, feel seasick.

THE EXPEDITION CONCLUDES IN PART THREE:

TO THE BRINK

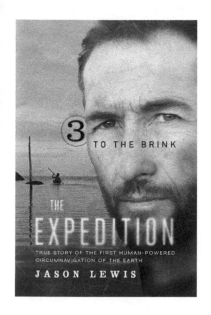

PART 3: *TO THE BRINK*

We re-join *The Expedition* for its third and final instalment with Jason, now seasoned explorer, and April, American schoolteacher at sea for the first time, battling to keep their pedal-powered boat *Moksha* from being dashed against Australia's Great Barrier Reef.

Crossing the infamous Coral Sea, they've endured gale force winds, rogue waves, and powerful currents pushing them off course for days at a time. On her thirtieth consecutive day of seasickness and now haemorrhaging blood, April is in urgent need of medical treatment. But in the uncharted waters north of Cape Flattery, far from coastguard assistance, there is little if any hope of rescue.

Even if they survive, Jason faces untold hazards to complete the first circumnavigation of the planet using only human power: waterless deserts, towering mountain ranges, seaborne pirates, and extremist hotspots. And there is still the overarching question he posed at the beginning, the one driving him forward that will take him *To The Brink* for an answer.

More at www.billyfishbooks.com

GLOSSARY OF NAUTICAL TERMS & BRITISH VERNACULAR

Admiralty chart	Nautical chart issued by the UK Hydrographic Office
Aft	Towards the rear of a boat
Amidships	The middle section of a ship
Barque	Square-rigged sailing ship
Becalmed	Unable to move due to lack of wind
Bilge pump	Pump for removing water from inside a boat
Biscuits	Cookies. Never serve with gravy
Blimey	Expression of surprise or disbelief, like wow, jeez, or hell
Bollocks	Expletive. Also testicles. Not to be confused with buttocks
Bollock-ache	A pain
Bosun	Ship's officer in charge of crew and equipment
Bow (sounding like cow)	Front end of a boat
Brackish	Mildly salty water
Breakwater	A barrier to protect a harbour from the force of waves
Budge up	Scoot over
Bugger that for a game of soldiers	To hell with that. Forget it
Buggery in a shrubbery	Sodomy in a bush. Not a shrub for keeping insects
Bulkhead	Partition between sections of a ship
Buoy	Anchored float used for mooring or marking navigation hazards
Caught a crab	Miss an oar or paddle stroke. Also consequence of night with call girl
Centreboard	Retractable keel giving stability to a boat
Christmas cracker	Decorated cardboard tube which, when pulled apart, emits a sharp crack and releases crappy toy

Clapped-out	Worn out
Cleat	T-shaped fixture for attaching a rope
Cutter	Coastal patrol boat
Doddle	Very easy
Dory	Usually follows hunky. Also flat-bottomed rowing boat
Eilbhe	Pronounced 'Elva'
Fodder	Food. Also father in New Jersey
Force (5, 6, 7, etc.)	Wind speed based on the Beaufort scale
Fore	Towards the front of a boat
Foredeck	Deck at the foremost part of a ship
Fortnight	Two weeks
Frangipani	Tropical shrub
Froggies	Derogatory name English use for the French, referring to their penchant for *cuisses de grenouille*, a dish featuring frogs' legs
Girl's Blouse	Sissy
Gunwales	Upper edge of a ship, formerly a support for cannon
Heel	Tilt over. Or a real ass
Hire	Rent
Holidaying	Vacationing
Hull	Main body of a boat
Jetty	Pier or wharf
Lava-lava	Sarong worn in Pacific region
Lee	Shelter
Leeward	Downwind
Lie-in	Sleep-in
Listing	Leaning over
Luff	Flap in wind
Make Fast	Secure firmly
Mayday	Radio distress signal
Neap tide	Moon phase when there is least difference between high and low water
Painter	Rope attached to the front of a boat used for tying to a wharf
Panhandle	Street beg
Penny Dropped	To finally realize something
Petrol	Gas

Physiotherapy	Physical therapy
Porridge	Oatmeal, a Goldilock's favourite
Port	Left side of a boat looking towards the bow
Punter	Customer. Also highly paid ball player doing very little
Putting the boot in	Give someone a hard time
Rashers	Bacon strips
Sea anchor	Device dragged through the water to slow a boat's drift
Sea shanty	Song sung by sailors. Not a shack by the sea
Shagging	Having sex. Also replacing '70s carpet
Shipwright	Boat builder
Shirty	Bad-tempered
Short-arsed	As in the editor of this book
Shroud	Part of a boat's rigging
Skipper	Captain. Also Gilligan's buddy
Skulduggery	Unscrupulous behaviour
Sod's Law	Murphy's Law
Sole boards	Cabin floor or lower decking
Southing	Distance travelled southwards
Starboard	Right side of a boat looking towards the bow
Stern	Rear end of a boat
Stopcock	Plug. Also command to rooster
Wind rose	Graphic illustrating average wind speed and direction at a particular place
Windscreen	Windshield

CONVERSIONS

1 pound sterling = 1.61 US dollars (approximate)
1 nautical mile = 1.151 statute miles
1 statute mile = 1.609 kilometres